Christmas
SWEETS

BARBOUR
PUBLISHING

Christmas
SWEETS

© 2003 by Barbour Publishing, Inc.

The contents of this book were written and compiled by Deborah Boone, Cathy Marie Hake, Amy Robertson, and Gail Sattler.

ISBN 1-59310-190-2

Published by Barbour Publishing, Inc., P.O. Box 719, Uhrichsville, Ohio 44683, www.barbourbooks.com

Our mission is to publish and distribute inspirational products offering exceptional value and biblical encouragement to the masses.

 Member of the
Evangelical Christian
Publishers Association

Printed in Italy.
5 4 3 2 1

Contents

Introduction

It's Christmastime—time for shopping and caroling, church services and family gatherings. . . With all the demands of the holiday season, how can you possibly find time to create delightfully delicious goodies for your Christmas guests *and* find time to relax and celebrate the real meaning of the Christmas season?

With recipes for bars and squares, candy and fudge, cookies galore, luscious cakes and breads, jar mixes, dips, tasty desserts, and more, *Christmas Sweets* will help you to satisfy the appetites of your family and friends and enhance your time together. Scriptures, quotations, and a bonus of two compact discs of traditional Christmas songs round out this holiday collection—helping you to remain in the Christmas spirit while you're cooking up tasty treats in the kitchen.

Christmas truly is the most wonderful time of the year. Make this year's celebration even more memorable with *Christmas Sweets.*

Christmas Brings Joy to Every Heart

Christmas brings joy to every heart,
Sets old and young rejoicing,
What angels sang once to all on earth,
Oh, hear the children voicing.
Bright is the tree with lights aglow,
Like birds that perch together,
The child that holdeth Christmas dear
Shall keep these joys forever.

Joy comes to the all the world today,
To halls and cottage hasting,
Come, sparrow and dove, from roof tree tall,
And share our Christmas feasting.
Dance, little child, on mother's knee,
The lovely day is dawning,
The road to paradise is found
The blessèd Christmas morning.

Once to this earth our Savior came,
An infant poor and lowly,
To open for us those gardens fair
Where dwell His angels holy.
Christmas joy He bringeth us,
The Christ child King of heaven,
"To every little child," He saith,
"Shall angel wings be given."

BERNHARDT S. INGEMANN

Bars and Squares

One day has left its mark in time

For all mankind to see;

It is the day when Christ was born—

That day made history.

D. DeHaan

Crispy PEANUT BUTTER BARS

½ stick butter or margarine
1 (10-ounce) bag miniature marshmallows
2 tablespoons peanut butter
6 cups crispy rice cereal

Grease a 9x13-inch pan; set aside. In a large microwave-safe bowl, combine the butter and marshmallows. Microwave on high (100%) for 3 minutes. Stir well. Add peanut butter and stir until well blended. Add rice cereal. Stir until evenly coated. Pour mixture into prepared pan. Let stand for 10 minutes. Cut into squares.

Cherry Cheese SQUARES

1 1/4 cups graham cracker crumbs
1/4 cup butter, melted
1 (8-ounce) package cream cheese, softened
1 cup powdered sugar
1/2 teaspoon vanilla extract
1 cup frozen whipped topping, thawed
1 (21-ounce) can cherry pie filling

Combine graham cracker crumbs and melted butter in an 8-inch square pan. Press into the bottom of the pan to form a crust. Chill in the refrigerator. In a large bowl, beat the cream cheese until fluffy; add the powdered sugar and vanilla; beat until smooth. Fold the whipped topping into the cream cheese mixture. Spread the mixture onto the chilled graham cracker crust and spoon cherry pie filling over it. Cover and place in the freezer. Before completely frozen, cut into small squares; return to the freezer. Remove from freezer 20–30 minutes before serving. Can be stored in the refrigerator.

NO-BAKE *Chocolate Oat* BARS

1 cup butter
$\frac{1}{2}$ cup brown sugar, packed
1 teaspoon vanilla extract
3 cups quick-cooking oats
1 cup semisweet chocolate chips
$\frac{1}{2}$ cup peanut butter

Lightly grease a 9-inch square pan; set aside. In a large saucepan, over medium heat, melt the butter. Stir in the brown sugar and vanilla. Mix in the oats. Cook over low heat for 2–3 minutes. Press half of the mixture into the bottom of the prepared pan. Reserve the other half for topping. Melt chocolate chips and peanut butter in the microwave until smooth. Pour the melted chocolate mixture over the layer in the pan, and spread evenly with the back of a spoon. Crumble the remaining oat mixture over the chocolate layer, pressing gently. Cover, and refrigerate overnight. Bring to room temperature before cutting into bars.

One Bowl BAR COOKIES

Pressed for time? This recipe doesn't take much time or cleanup.

> 1 package applesauce-raisin cake mix
> ¾ cup quick oats
> ¼ cup wheat germ
> ½ cup light molasses
> ¼ cup orange juice
> 2 eggs
> 2 tablespoons vegetable oil
> ½ cup raisins
> ½ cup flaked coconut

Combine cake mix, oats, and wheat germ. Add molasses, orange juice, eggs, and oil. Stir until well blended, then add raisins and coconut. Spread in greased jelly roll pan. Bake at 375° for 20 minutes (lightly browned and pulled away from pan's edge). Cool. Ice with Orange Glaze before cutting.

Orange Glaze:

> 2 cups confectioners' sugar   ¼–⅓ cup orange juice

Blend together until thin enough to pour but thick enough to spread.

Apricot SQUARES

9 apricots, halved and pitted
1 cup butter or margarine, divided
$^1/_3$ cup firmly packed brown sugar
9 maraschino cherries
1 cup sugar
2 large eggs
2 cups cake flour, divided
2 teaspoons baking powder
$^1/_2$ teaspoon salt
1 teaspoon grated lemon rind
$^2/_3$ cup milk

Cut each apricot half into four slices. Melt $\frac{1}{4}$ cup butter and pour into bottom of 9-inch square pan. Sprinkle brown sugar evenly over butter. Arrange cherries and half the apricot slices in sugar mixture. Chop remaining apricot slices; set aside. Beat sugar, eggs, and remaining $\frac{3}{4}$ cup butter. Add in 1 cup of the flour, baking powder, salt, and lemon rind. Gradually beat in remaining flour alternately with milk until batter is smooth. Stir in reserved chopped apricots. Carefully spoon batter over apricots in pan. Bake at 350° for 45–50 minutes or until cake springs back when top is lightly touched with finger. Remove from oven and place serving plate facedown over cake. Turn upside down to unmold. Cut into squares. Serve warm or at room temperature. Makes 9 squares.

It is good to be children sometimes,

and never better than at Christmas,

when its mighty Founder

was a child Himself.

CHARLES DICKENS, *A Christmas Carol*

Brown Sugar CHEWS

1 egg
1 cup packed brown sugar
1 teaspoon vanilla
$\frac{1}{2}$ cup sifted flour
$\frac{1}{4}$ teaspoon salt
$\frac{1}{4}$ teaspoon baking soda
1 cup chopped walnuts

Stir together egg, brown sugar, and vanilla. Add flour, salt, and baking soda. Fold in walnuts. Bake at 350° for 18–20 minutes in well-greased 8x8-inch pan. Should be soft when removed from the oven. Cool in pan, then cut into squares.

No-Bake

PEANUT CHOCOLATE BROWNIES

4 cups graham cracker crumbs
1 cup peanuts, chopped
$\frac{1}{2}$ cup powdered sugar
$\frac{1}{4}$ cup peanut butter
2 cups semisweet chocolate chips
1 cup evaporated milk
1 teaspoon vanilla extract

Grease a 9-inch square pan; set aside. In a medium bowl, combine the graham cracker crumbs, peanuts, powdered sugar, and peanut butter with a pastry blender. In a small saucepan, over low heat, melt the chocolate chips with the evaporated milk, stirring constantly. Remove from heat and stir in the vanilla. Remove $\frac{1}{2}$ cup of the melted chocolate mixture and set aside. Pour the remaining chocolate mixture over the graham cracker crumb mixture and stir until well blended. Spread evenly in the prepared pan. Frost with the reserved chocolate mixture. Chill in the refrigerator for at least 1 hour.

Frosted OATMEAL SQUARES

2 cups quick oats
½ cup firmly packed brown sugar
½ cup softened butter or margarine
¼ cup light corn syrup
3 ounces (½ cup) semisweet chocolate chips
⅓ cup chunky peanut butter

Mix oats, brown sugar, butter, and corn syrup. Press mixture evenly in a 12x8-inch glass baking dish and microwave on high for 3½–4 minutes or until bubbly over entire top. Cool. Melt chocolate and peanut butter for approximately 1 minute, stirring halfway through. Mix until smooth. Spread on cooled oatmeal mixture. Chill and cut into squares.

Cherry CHA-CHA

Crust:

  ½ cup butter   2 cups graham wafer
  ¼ cup sugar   crumbs

Melt butter. Stir in sugar and crumbs. Save ⅓ for topping. Press into a greased 9x13-inch pan. Bake at 350° for 10 minutes. Cool.

Filling:

  2 cups whipping cream   1 19-ounce can cherry
  4 cups small marshmallows   pie filling

Whip cream and fold in marshmallows. Spread half on crust. Spoon pie filling on top and smooth. Spread other half of cream mixture on top of pie filling. Sprinkle crumbs on top. Chill for several hours. Cut into 12 pieces.

Come to Bethlehem and see

Him whose birth the angels sing;

Come adore on bended knee

Christ the Lord, the newborn King.

TRADITIONAL FRENCH CAROL

Chocolate TRIO SQUARES

These only sound complicated—
they go together fast and look impressive.

LAYER 1:

Cream together and spread in greased and floured 9x9-inch pan:
    ¼ cup butter   1 cup sifted flour
    ¼ teaspoon salt

Bake at 350° for 15 minutes.

LAYER 2:

2 eggs $\frac{1}{4}$ cup brown sugar

Beat together well, then add:

1 cup finely chopped   2 tablespoons flour
   walnuts $\frac{1}{2}$ cup shredded coconut
1 teaspoon vanilla $\frac{1}{4}$ teaspoon salt

Spread over first baked layer. Bake at 350° for 15 minutes. Cool in pan.

LAYER 3 (ICING):

1 cup semisweet   1 tablespoon water
   chocolate chips   Chopped nuts
$\frac{1}{4}$ cup light corn syrup

Melt chocolate chips in microwave; add $\frac{1}{4}$ cup light corn syrup and 1 tablespoon water. Spread over second layer. Sprinkle with chopped nuts if desired.

Frosted PEANUT SQUARES

½ cup firmly packed brown sugar
½ cup peanut butter
½ cup corn syrup
1 cup roughly chopped peanuts
4 cups cornflakes
1 cup melted chocolate chips

Combine brown sugar, peanut butter, and corn syrup in large saucepan. Cook over medium heat until mixture starts to bubble, stirring constantly. Remove from heat; stir in peanuts and cornflakes, using two forks to mix thoroughly. Press warm mixture evenly and firmly into buttered 13x9-inch rectangular pan. Spread roughly with melted chocolate chips and cool. Cut into squares when firm. Yield: 24 2-inch squares.

 _Lemon_ BARS

(From the kitchen of Angela Boone-Guzman)

Crust:

    ½ cup butter   1 cup flour
    ¼ cup powdered sugar

Cream butter and sugar until fluffy. Add flour and mix well. Spread in 8x8-inch greased pan. Bake at 350° for 12 minutes.

Second layer:

    1 cup sugar   ¼ teaspoon salt
    2 beaten eggs   2 tablespoons flour
    4 tablespoons lemon juice   ½ teaspoon baking powder

Beat sugar and eggs, adding in lemon juice. Add dry ingredients and mix well. Spread over crust, covering all edges. Bake at 350° for 30 minutes. Cool and dust with powdered sugar. Cut in 1x2-inch rectangles.

Tip: _Angela's Swedish great-grandmother substituted potato flour for the wheat flour and always creamed the butter for a full 5 minutes until it was light and fluffy._

Dream BARS

Base:

    1 1/2 cups flour
    1/2 cup butter, softened
    1/2 cup firmly packed
      brown sugar

Blend the above ingredients until crumbly. Press into an ungreased 13x9-inch baking pan. Bake at 350° for 12 minutes.

Filling:

    3 eggs
    1 1/2 cups firmly packed
      brown sugar
    Pinch salt
    1 1/2 cups shredded
      unsweetened coconut
    1/4 cup flour
    1 teaspoon baking
      powder
    1 teaspoon vanilla
    1 cup chopped walnuts

Beat eggs and 1 1/2 cups brown sugar for 2 minutes at highest speed of an electric mixer. Blend in remaining ingredients at low speed. Pour and spread over partially baked crust. Bake at 350° for 20–30 minutes, until deep golden brown. Cool. Cut into bars using a knife dipped in hot water.

They are more precious than gold,
than much pure gold;
they are sweeter than honey,
than honey from the comb.

<small>PSALM</small> 19:10

 PINEAPPLE SQUARES

Crust:

4 cups flour   1 cup sour cream
1 pound butter

Mix flour and butter. Add sour cream and refrigerate for 2 hours.

Filling:

2 tins crushed pineapple,   3–4 tablespoons cornstarch
    including juice   1 cup sugar

Topping:

Icing sugar

Combine the above filling mix and cook until thickened. Let cool. Roll
half the dough onto jelly roll pan. Spread with cooled filling. Top with
remaining dough. Pierce top of dough with fork. Bake at 325° for approximately 50 minutes. Cool and sprinkle with icing sugar.

Gingersnap BARS

³/₄ cup shortening
1 cup sugar
1 teaspoon cinnamon
¹/₂ teaspoon ginger
¹/₄ cup molasses
2 cups all-purpose flour

2 teaspoons baking soda
¹/₂ teaspoon cloves
¹/₂ teaspoon salt
1 egg
2 tablespoons sugar

Melt shortening in large saucepan; cool 5 minutes. Add remaining ingredients except 2 tablespoons sugar; mix well. Press in bottom of greased 15x10-inch jelly roll pan. Sprinkle with remaining sugar. Bake at 375° for 10–12 minutes. Do not overbake. After 5 minutes, cut into bars. Cool completely.

GRAHAM *Napoleons*

57–60 graham wafers, whole
2 small packages cream cheese
2 packages instant vanilla pudding mix
4 cups cold milk
$^1/_2$ cup whipping cream, whipped
1 envelope unflavored gelatin
$^1/_4$ cup water
1 cup fresh or frozen strawberries, chopped
1 cup icing sugar
2 tablespoons milk
2 tablespoons strawberry jam, melted

Line bottom of 13x9-inch pan with wafers to cover bottom of pan. Beat 4 cups milk with pudding mix for 2 minutes. Set aside. Beat cream cheese until fluffy, fold into pudding mix, then fold in whipped cream. Take 3 ½ cups of this mixture and set aside. Soften gelatin in ¼ cup water for 5 minutes. Dissolve over low heat, stirring constantly. Mix gelatin into strawberries and fold into remaining pudding mixture. Pour strawberry mixture evenly into prepared pan. Top with another layer of wafers, then pour reserved vanilla cream mixture over this. Top with remaining wafers and refrigerate until set. Top with glaze made from icing sugar and 2 tablespoons milk. Do not allow icing to set. While the icing is still drippy, pipe or drizzle straight lines of melted jam over the icing. Draw the tip of a knife or a toothpick through the lines to make a pleasing pattern. Makes 18 bars.

Danish APPLE BARS

2 ½ cups flour	4 cups diced and peeled apples
1 teaspoon salt	1 cup sugar
1 cup shortening	1 teaspoon cinnamon
1 egg, separated	1 cup icing sugar
Milk	2 tablespoons water
1 cup crushed cornflakes	1 teaspoon vanilla

Sift the flour and salt. Cut in shortening until coarse. Set egg white aside. Beat egg yolk slightly. Add enough milk to the egg yolk to make ⅔ cup. Slowly add egg/milk mixture to flour mixture until it resembles pie dough. Divide dough in half. Roll one portion into rectangle to fit jelly roll pan and bring up on sides. Sprinkle crushed cornflakes on top of crust. Set aside. Sprinkle apples with sugar and cinnamon, then spread apples over the cornflakes. Roll out remaining dough to fit over apples. Moisten edges with milk and seal. Beat egg white until stiff. Brush over top crust. Bake at 350° for approximately 1 hour. Combine icing sugar, water, and vanilla. Spread over top while still warm.

*At that time Mary got ready and hurried
to a town in the hill country of Judea,
where she entered Zechariah's home
and greeted Elizabeth.
When Elizabeth heard Mary's greeting,
the baby leaped in her womb,
and Elizabeth was filled
with the Holy Spirit.
In a loud voice she exclaimed:
"Blessed are you among women,
and blessed is the child you will bear!"*

LUKE 1:39–42

King Gustav COOKIES

2 sticks of butter, softened
1 cup sugar
1 large egg, divided into yolk
    and egg white

1 cup all-purpose flour
1 teaspoon imitation
    brandy extract
Diced, sliced, or
    chopped pecans

First cream butter with mixer. Gradually add granulated sugar a little at a time; cream well. Add egg yolk and cream with above; add sifted flour a little at a time. Add extract. Divide dough evenly in 2 parts and lightly grease 2 16x11x1-inch pans all over. Put dough on pans, and spread evenly, quite thin (12–13 ounces each pan). Put some of the egg white on top of each batter, rubbing the egg white on top of each batter with the palm of the hand. Pour off excess egg white (egg white should be moved around the top of the batter until smooth and shiny). Sprinkle pecans over batter. Bake 55 minutes at 250° (preheated oven), or at 325° for 15–20 minutes. Check after 25 minutes, as cookies bake faster in a gas oven. Cookies should be a light brownish color before removing from oven. Cut into squares as soon as cookies are removed from oven. Let cool for 1 hour before removing cookies from pan.

Marshmallow DREAM SQUARES

½ package graham wafers, crushed
⅓ package miniature marshmallows
½ cup chopped dates
¼ cup fine coconut or nuts
½ cup melted butter
½ cup brown sugar
1 egg

Mix together graham wafers, marshmallows, dates, and coconut/nuts. Melt butter and brown sugar together. Beat in egg and mix. Combine with rest of mixed ingredients. Pack into buttered pan. Refrigerate. Cover with your favorite butter icing, if desired.

Rainbow BARS

Base:

    $\frac{1}{2}$ cup butter   2 tablespoons sugar

    2 cups flour

Mix well. Spread in 9x12-inch pan. Bake for 15 minutes at 350°.

Filling:

    3 tablespoons cornstarch   1 tin crushed pineapple,

    $\frac{1}{2}$ cup maraschino cherries, cut up   with juice

    1 teaspoon almond flavoring $\frac{1}{2}$ cup sugar

Mix the cornstarch with cherry juice to make a paste, and mix all filling ingredients. Cook about 15 minutes until thick. Pour on top of base while both are still hot.

Topping:

    3 egg whites   3 tablespoons sugar

    1 teaspoon vanilla   Pinch salt

    Coconut (optional)

Beat well and spread on cake. Sprinkle with coconut, if desired, and bake at 350° until topping is brown.

Cherry Banana SLICE

10 ounces margarine
6 ounces caster sugar
3 large eggs
6 ounces self-rising flour
1 teaspoon baking powder
2 bananas, peeled and mashed (separately)
1 lemon, rind and juice, divided
8 ounces sifted icing sugar
4 glacé cherries, halved

Beat 6 ounces margarine with sugar, eggs, flour, and baking powder. Add 1 banana, lemon rind, and 1 tablespoon juice and beat until smooth. Bake in greased 9-inch square pan at 375° for 50 minutes. Cool. Set aside. Mix remaining banana with 1 teaspoon lemon juice. Set aside. Cream rest of margarine with icing sugar and remaining lemon juice. Reserve half; mix chopped banana into one half. Trim edges of the cake and cut in half; sandwich halves together with banana icing. Spread a third of the remaining icing over top of cake. Put remaining icing in a piping bag fitted with a star nozzle. Pipe swirls round top of cake, then decorate with halved cherries.

Cottage CHEESECAKE SQUARES

These squares are low in sugar and fat!

Crust:

1 cup graham cracker crumbs   1 teaspoon cinnamon
3 tablespoons melted butter

Filling:

1¼ pounds solid curd (pressed)   2 eggs
     cottage cheese   1 teaspoon vanilla
½ cup sugar

Topping:

1 cup unflavored yogurt   ¼ teaspoon vanilla
2 tablespoons sugar   12 strawberries, halved,
                     fresh or frozen

To make crust: Mix all 3 ingredients and press firmly into 8x8-inch pan.

To make filling: Beat cottage cheese and sugar until smooth, or blend in food processor blender. Add eggs, one at a time, and beat in vanilla. Pour over crust and bake at 350° for 25–30 minutes or until filling begins to puff slightly. Do not allow to brown. Remove from oven and let rest for 5 minutes.

To make topping: Combine yogurt, sugar, and vanilla. Spoon evenly over cheesecake. Return to oven for 5 minutes. Allow to cool to room temperature, then refrigerate overnight. Cut into 24 squares and top each piece with a strawberry half. Serve chilled.

*"Therefore I tell you,
do not worry about your life,
what you will eat or drink;
or about your body, what you will wear.
Is not life more important than food,
and the body more important than clothes?"*

MATTHEW 6:25

Peanut Butter BARS

$^{1}/_{2}$ cup sugar
$^{1}/_{2}$ cup light corn syrup
1 cup peanut butter
1 teaspoon vanilla
2 cups cornflake cereal
1 cup Rice Krispies cereal
$^{1}/_{3}$ cup brown sugar
$^{1}/_{4}$ cup cream

Heat sugar and corn syrup until sugar melts. Add peanut butter and vanilla. Mix and add cereals. Heat again and pack into a greased 9x9-inch pan. Boil brown sugar and cream together for 2 minutes (will be thin). Pour on cake. Allow to set when cool.

Chewy CHOCOLATE BARS

$^3/_4$ cup honey
1 cup peanut butter
1 cup semisweet chocolate chips
$1^1/_2$ cups miniature marshmallows
3 cups crispy rice cereal
1 cup salted peanuts

In a large saucepan over medium heat, melt the honey and peanut butter. Bring to a boil. Stir in chocolate chips and marshmallows. Stir until smooth. Add the cereal and peanuts. Blend well and remove from heat. Pour into a lightly greased 9x13-inch pan. Press firmly with a spatula. Let stand for 10 minutes. Cut into bars before hardening.

Butterscotch SQUARES

$^1/_1$ cup butter
1 cup packed brown sugar
1 egg
$^1/_2$ teaspoon vanilla
1 cup flour
1 teaspoon baking powder
$^1/_2$ cup blanched almond halves

Cream butter, brown sugar, egg, and vanilla. Sift dry ingredients. Add dry ingredients into mixture. Spread in greased 8x8-inch pan. Top with almonds. Bake at 350° for 30–35 minutes. Cool, then cut into squares.

"Do not be afraid.
I bring you good news of great joy
that will be for all the people.
Today in the town of David a Savior
has been born to you;
he is Christ the Lord.
This will be a sign to you:
You will find a baby wrapped in cloths
and lying in a manger."

LUKE 2:10–12

Cream Cheese BARS

Like cheesecake? These are a dream!

1 stick butter
1 box golden yellow cake mix
1 pound box confectioners' sugar
2 eggs
1 package (8 ounces) cream cheese

Mix butter and cake mix until crumbly. Spread in buttered 9x13-inch pan. Cream confectioners' sugar, eggs, and cream cheese. Spread over cake mix crust. Bake at 350° for 35 minutes. Watch carefully—these bars burn easily.

 SQUARES

2 eggs
1 cup brown sugar
2 teaspoons vanilla
1 teaspoon baking powder
1 cup cake flour
$\frac{1}{2}$ teaspoon salt
$\frac{2}{3}$ cup chopped nuts
1 cup candied fruit, chopped
1 cup dried fruit (dates, citron, raisins,
    figs) chopped

Beat eggs until they start to stiffen. Gradually beat in sugar and add vanilla. Sift dry ingredients together and add. Fold in chopped nuts and the fruit. Pour in 8x8-inch pan that is generously sprayed with nonstick spray. Bake at 350° for 30–40 minutes. Remove from pan while warm. Cool and cut into 1-inch squares.

Smoothie SQUARES

1 package graham wafers (whole)
1 large package vanilla pudding
   (cooked, not instant)
2 cups milk
1 ½ cups whipping cream
1 cup icing sugar
1 tablespoon butter
1–2 tablespoons milk
1 square semisweet chocolate

Line a 9x13-inch pan with graham wafers. Cook vanilla pudding with milk and spread over wafers. Cool. Whip cream and spread over pudding. Cover with graham wafers. Prepare icing by beating icing sugar, butter, and enough milk to make the texture thin but not too liquidy. Glaze over top layer of graham wafers. Swirl in melted chocolate.

Mint SWIRL BARS

Bars:

1 3-ounce package cream cheese

¼ cup butter (do not use margarine)

¾ cup sugar

2 eggs

⅔ cup flour

½ teaspoon baking powder

½ teaspoon salt

⅓ cup chopped walnuts

1 1-ounce square semisweet chocolate,
   melted

½ teaspoon peppermint extract

2–3 drops green food coloring

Glaze:

1 1-ounce square semisweet chocolate
1 tablespoon butter
1 cup icing sugar
$\frac{1}{2}$ teaspoon vanilla
2–3 tablespoons boiling water

Beat cream cheese, butter, and sugar. Add eggs, one at a time, beating well after each addition. Combine flour, powder, and salt; mix well. Transfer half of the batter to another bowl; set aside. To half of mixture, stir in nuts and chocolate. Spread in greased 9-inch square pan. To other half, stir in peppermint extract and food coloring. Spoon over chocolate layer and cut with a knife to swirl. Bake at 350° for 15–20 minutes until toothpick comes out clean. Cool on wire rack. Melt chocolate and butter, remove from heat, then stir in icing sugar, vanilla, and enough water to achieve a glaze consistency. Pour over cooled cake and spread evenly. Cut into bars. Makes 2 dozen.

Cranberry CRUNCH SQUARES

1 (16-ounce) can jellied cranberry sauce
2 ⅓ cups rolled oats
¾ cup all-purpose flour
1 ⅝ cups packed brown sugar
1 cup butter, melted

Spread the cranberry sauce into the bottom of a greased 9x13-inch baking pan. Stir oats, flour, brown sugar, and butter until the mixture resembles coarse crumbs. Sprinkle crumb mixture over cranberry sauce. Bake at 350° for 25 minutes. Cool and cut into squares.

 *Frosted* BANANA BARS

(From the kitchen of Vickie McDonough)

½ cup butter or margarine, softened	2 cups all-purpose flour
1 ½ cups sugar	1 teaspoon baking soda
2 eggs	¼ teaspoon salt
1 cup (8 ounces) sour cream	2 medium ripe bananas,
1 teaspoon vanilla extract	mashed (about 1 cup)

In a mixing bowl, cream butter and sugar. Add eggs, sour cream, and vanilla. Combine flour, baking soda, and salt; gradually add to the creamed mixture. Stir in bananas. Spread into a greased 15x10x1-inch baking pan. Bake at 350° for 20–25 minutes or until a toothpick inserted near the center comes out clean. Cool.

Frosting:

1 package (8 ounces)	2 teaspoons vanilla extract
cream cheese, softened	3 ¾–4 cups powdered
½ cup butter or margarine	sugar

In a mixing bowl beat cream cheese, butter, and vanilla. Gradually beat in enough powdered sugar to achieve desired consistency. Frost bars. Store in the refrigerator.

*Almond* SQUARES

Base:

1 ½ cups flour
½ cup butter
2 tablespoons icing sugar

Bend and press into a 9-inch square pan. Bake for 10 minutes at 350°.

Filling:

4 tablespoons butter
1 cup brown sugar
¼ cup sour cream
1 ½ cups slivered almonds
1 ½ cups slivered almonds

Boil first 4 ingredients for 3 minutes. Add slivered almonds. Spread over base and bake for 10 minutes at 350°.

Christmas CANDY BARS

1 cup sugar
1 cup light corn syrup
1 ½ cups creamy peanut butter
6 cups rice flakes cereal
6 ounces milk chocolate chips
6 ounces butterscotch chips

Grease a 9x13-inch pan; set aside. In a medium saucepan, bring sugar and corn syrup to a boil. Stir in the peanut butter; batter will be stiff. Mix in the cereal. Press into prepared pan. In a small microwave-safe bowl, add chocolate chips and butterscotch chips. Microwave on high (100%) at 15-second intervals until completely melted. Spread over the cereal mixture. Allow to set at room temperature until cool. Cut into bars.

*When they had seen him,
they spread the word
concerning what had been
told them about this child,
and all who heard it were amazed
at what the shepherds said to them.*

LUKE 2:17–18

Dreamy APRICOT SQUARES

1 cup crushed graham wafer crumbs
1 cup sifted all-purpose flour
1 cup shredded coconut
½ teaspoon salt
1 cup melted butter
1 cup dried apricots
2 eggs
1 cup brown sugar
1 teaspoon lemon juice
⅓ cup sifted flour
½ teaspoon baking powder
¼ teaspoon salt

Combine crumbs, flour, coconut, and salt. Add melted butter and mix. Reserve 1 cup for topping. Pack remainder in 9x9-inch pan. Bake for 10 minutes at 350°. Chop apricots and cover with water. Simmer until tender, approximately 15 minutes, and drain. Beat eggs until light and add brown sugar and lemon juice. Stir in dry ingredients and spread over bottom. Layer and sprinkle with reserved cup for topping. Bake for 30–35 minutes at 350°. Cool and cut into squares.

 SLICE

1 cup soft butter or margarine
1 ½ cups sugar
4 eggs
1 teaspoon vanilla
2 teaspoons almond flavoring
3 cups flour
1 can cherry pie filling

Cream butter and sugar. Add 1 egg at a time, mixing well after each addition. Add flavorings. Add flour, 1 cup at a time, mixing well. Batter will be very soft; do not add more flour. Spread ⅔ of the batter in bottom of greased 15x10-inch jelly roll pan. Spread on can of pie filling (in such a way that you will leave small spaces with no pie filling). Spread on remaining ⅓ of batter. Bake at 350° for 30–40 minutes, or until golden. Sprinkle with icing sugar when cool.

Penuche SQUARES

Base:

½ cup butter	1 teaspoon vanilla
½ cup sugar	1 cup cake flour
2 egg yolks	1 teaspoon baking powder

Topping:

2 egg whites	1 cup walnuts
1 cup brown sugar	

Cream butter and sugar together. Add egg yolks and vanilla and then dry ingredients. Press into 9x9-inch greased pan. Set aside. Beat egg whites until stiff, but not dry, and gradually add brown sugar. Fold in walnuts. Bake at 325° for approximately 35 minutes.

Brownies

1 cup sugar
$^1/_2$ cup butter
2 eggs
$^1/_2$ cup milk
$^2/_3$ cup sifted flour

$^1/_2$ teaspoon baking powder
1 cup nut meats
2 squares baking chocolate
1 teaspoon vanilla

Mix ingredients in the order given. Pour into greased pan. Bake at 350°
for 25 minutes.

Icing:

1 cup brown sugar
$1^1/_2$ tablespoons butter
Pinch of salt
$^1/_4$ cup milk

$1^1/_2$ cups powdered sugar
1 teaspoon vanilla
2 tablespoons cocoa

Combine brown sugar, butter, salt, and milk. Bring to boil and cook
slowly for 3 minutes. Cool to lukewarm. Add powdered sugar, vanilla,
and cocoa. Beat until smooth and spreadable.

No-Bake GRANOLA BARS

2 ½ cups crisp rice cereal
2 cups quick-cooking oats
½ cup raisins
½ cup brown sugar, firmly packed
½ cup light corn syrup
½ cup peanut butter
1 teaspoon vanilla extract
½ cup milk chocolate chips

In a large bowl, combine crisp rice cereal, oats, and raisins; set aside. In a small saucepan, over medium heat, bring the brown sugar and corn syrup to a boil, stirring constantly. Remove from heat and stir in peanut butter and vanilla until well blended. Pour the peanut butter mixture over the cereal mixture and toss until well coated. Let stand for 10 minutes. Stir in the chocolate chips. Press the mixture into a 9x13-inch pan. Allow to cool completely before cutting into bars.

Christians, Lo, the Star Appeareth

Christians, lo, the star appeareth;
Lo 'tis yet Messiah's day;
Still with tribute treasure laden
Come the wise men on their way.

Where a life is spent in service,
Walking where the Master trod,
There is scattered myrrh most fragrant
For the blessèd Christ of God.

JAMES A. BLAISDELL

Breads and Fruitcakes

The Christmas Gift

The Christmas Season speaks to us of peace
A season of solace and joy.
When eager children must wait endless hours
To examine their new Christmas toys.
The family will gather for breaking of bread
Thanking God for their bountiful food,
Then thanking each other for gifts they exchanged
As they bask in a joyful mood.
However, most cherished of all of their gifts
Is a gift they can't visibly see.
This endowment is offered to one and to all
But is not to be found 'neath the tree.
It's a blessing bestowed to all of mankind
God Himself is in it reflected
It carries the power to alter his life,
If man simply opts to accept it.
This gift is the reason we celebrate
On Christmas the wee infant's birth
For God has appeared in a human form
To walk among men on the earth.

AUTHOR UNKNOWN

Classic Christmas FRUITCAKE

1 pound dark raisins
1 pound mixed fruit
3 pineapple rings
2 pounds sultana raisins
1 pound glazed cherries
1 pound mixed peel
1 pound blanched almonds
3½ cups flour
1 pound butter
1 pound sugar

12 eggs
1 teaspoon baking soda
2 ounces unsweetened chocolate
1 cup grape jelly
1 teaspoon salt
1 teaspoon nutmeg
1 teaspoon cloves
1 teaspoon allspice
2 tablespoons cinnamon

Pour boiling water on raisins and let sit for a few minutes. Drain and dry. Cover fruits and almonds with 1 cup of flour. Mix well. Cream butter and sugar; add eggs one at a time and beat. Add melted chocolate and softened jelly. Sift together remaining flour, soda, salt, and spices. Add to fruit and mix well. Put 2 layers of brown paper (greased) in loaf tins and pour in batter. Bake at 275° for 4–5 hours. For smaller loaf pans, bake for only 2½ hours. Cool 5 minutes and remove from pans.

Banana Nut BREAD

4 cups all-purpose flour
1¼ cups nonfat dry milk
4 teaspoons baking powder
1 teaspoon cinnamon
4 large eggs
3½ cups ripe bananas, mashed
2 cups sugar
1 cup vegetable oil
1 cup chopped walnuts

Preheat oven to 350°. Grease two 9x5-inch loaf pans. Stir together flour, dry milk, baking powder, and cinnamon in a medium bowl. In a large mixing bowl, add the eggs, bananas, sugar, and oil. With an electric hand mixer on medium speed, beat the banana mixture until it is completely blended. Gradually beat in the flour mixture. Stir in the walnuts. Spoon the mixture into prepared loaf pans. Bake for 60–65 minutes or until toothpick inserted in center comes out clean. Cool in pans for 10 minutes. Remove to wire racks to cool completely.

Chocolate Chip PUMPKIN BREAD

3 cups powdered sugar
1 (15-ounce) can solid-pack pumpkin
1 cup vegetable oil
²/₃ cup water
4 eggs
3¹/₂ cups all-purpose flour
1 tablespoon ground cinnamon
1 tablespoon ground nutmeg
2 teaspoons baking soda
1¹/₂ teaspoons salt
1 cup miniature semisweet chocolate chips
¹/₂ cup walnuts, chopped (optional)

Preheat oven to 350°. Grease and flour three 1-pound-size coffee cans or three 9x5-inch loaf pans. In a large bowl, combine sugar, pumpkin, oil, water, and eggs. Beat until smooth. Blend in flour, cinnamon, nutmeg, baking soda, and salt. Fold in chocolate chips and nuts. Fill cans or loaf pans ¹/₂–³/₄ full. Bake for 1 hour or until a toothpick inserted in the center comes out clean. Cool on wire racks before removing from cans or loaf pans. Makes 3 loaves.

Gumdrop CAKE

1 cup dates
1 package raisins
1 cup butter
$\frac{1}{2}$ cup water
2 cups flour
2 eggs
1 teaspoon cinnamon
1 cup brown sugar
1 pound gumdrops, cut up (no black ones!)
1 cup sweetened applesauce
1 teaspoon baking soda
Nuts (optional)

Boil dates, raisins, butter, and water. Let cool. Add other ingredients. Bake at 350° for 1½ hours.

Cinnamon Swirl LOAF

1 cup sour cream
1 teaspoon baking soda
$^{1}/_{2}$ cup butter
1 cup sugar
2 eggs
1 teaspoon vanilla
1$^{3}/_{4}$ cups flour
1 teaspoon baking powder
$^{1}/_{2}$ cup brown sugar
1$^{1}/_{2}$ tablespoons cinnamon

Mix sour cream and baking soda together and allow to stand while mixing rest of loaf. Blend butter, sugar, eggs, and vanilla together. Beat until fluffy. Mix flour and baking powder together. Add flour mixture to butter mixture alternately with sour cream. In a separate bowl, mix the brown sugar and cinnamon. Put $^{1}/_{3}$ of the batter into a greased 9x5x3 loaf pan; spread cinnamon mixture and repeat to form layers. Then swirl with a knife. Bake for approximately 1 hour at 350°.

*Taste and see that
the LORD is good.*

PSALM 34:8

 BREAD

⅓ cup butter or margarine, softened	2 tablespoons flour
¾ cup sugar	¼ teaspoon salt
1 teaspoon baking soda	1½ cups apples, peeled and chopped
1 tablespoon lemon juice	1 teaspoon cinnamon
2 eggs	1½ cups flour
1 teaspoon vanilla extract	2 tablespoons sugar
	2 tablespoons butter

Preheat oven to 325°. Grease and flour a 9x5-inch loaf pan; set aside. In a small bowl, cream together butter and sugar. In a separate bowl, dissolve baking soda in lemon juice. Mix in eggs and vanilla. Beat butter mixture and egg mixture together. Add flour and salt. Be careful not to overmix. Gently stir in apples. In a small bowl, add cinnamon, 2 tablespoons flour, and 2 tablespoons sugar. Cut in 2 tablespoons butter to get a coarse crumb mixture; set aside. Spoon ½ apple batter into prepared loaf pan. Sprinkle with ½ crumb mixture. Spoon in remaining batter and sprinkle with remaining crumb mixture. Press crumbs gently into surface of batter. Bake for 80–90 minutes or until a toothpick inserted in the center comes out clean. Cool for 10 minutes in pan before turning out onto a wire rack. Allow to cool completely before slicing.

Mount Vernon RAISIN FRUITCAKE

2 cups sultana raisins
1 cup glacé cherries, halved
2 cups candied pineapple, diced
Orange juice (enough to cover fruit)
1 cup butter
2 cups sugar
5 eggs, well beaten
3 cups flour
1 1/2 teaspoons baking powder
1 teaspoon salt
2 cups pecans

Combine the first three fruits with juice; mix well. Cover and set aside overnight. Next day, cream butter; add sugar and beat until light and fluffy. Then add beaten eggs and blend mixture together. Sift flour, baking powder, and salt together and stir into batter. Pour this batter over fruit mixture and stir in the pecans. Mix until fruits are well blended. Pour batter into foil or parchment paper lined 10- or 11-inch tube pan. Bake at 300° for 2 1/2–3 hours, or until a cake tester inserted in the center comes out clean. Cool cake for 1/2 hour, then remove foil or paper and let cake cool. When thoroughly cool, wrap cake in foil and allow cake to ripen for at least three weeks before serving.

No-Bake FRUITCAKE

1 cup pecans, chopped
1 cup raisins, chopped
1 cup walnuts, chopped
1 (4-ounce) jar maraschino cherries, drained
    and chopped
1 (14-ounce) can sweetened condensed milk
1 (12-ounce) package vanilla wafers, crushed

In a medium bowl, combine the pecans, raisins, walnuts, cherries, sweetened condensed milk, and vanilla wafers. The dough will be thick; use your hands to get it completely mixed. Shape the dough into a ring on top of a dinner plate. Wrap the cake and plate in many layers of plastic wrap. Refrigerate the cake for at least a week to allow the flavors to blend and all of the milk to be absorbed.

Date LOAF

1 teaspoon baking soda
1 cup chopped dates
1 cup boiling water
1 teaspoon butter
1 cup sugar
1 teaspoon vanilla
1 egg
2 cups flour
1 teaspoon baking powder
$\frac{1}{2}$ cup chopped walnuts

Sprinkle soda on dates; add boiling water and let stand. When cool, add butter, sugar, vanilla, beaten egg, then dry ingredients. Bake in 325° oven for 1 hour or until a toothpick comes out clean when poked into loaf.

Blueberry Orange LOAF

$1/2$ teaspoon baking soda
2 teaspoons baking powder
2 cups flour
$3/4$ cup sugar
$1/4$ teaspoon salt
1 tablespoon grated orange rind
$1/4$ cup orange juice
$1/4$ cup butter, melted
$3/4$ cup milk
1 egg, beaten
1 cup fresh or frozen blueberries, drained
  and dried
$1/2$ cup chopped nuts

Sift first five ingredients (dry ingredients) into a bowl. Combine the next five ingredients and stir into the flour mixture. Beat well. Grease a 9x5x3-inch loaf pan and spread with $1/3$ batter. Sprinkle with half the blueberries and nuts. Add another third of batter and remaining fruit and nuts. Add remaining batter. Bake at 350° for approximately 50 minutes.

Cinnamon CRESCENT ROLLS

1 (8-ounce) can refrigerated crescent roll dough
¾ cup cinnamon chips
⅓ cup powdered sugar
½ tablespoon ground cinnamon

Preheat oven to 375°. Unroll dough and separate into triangles. Sprinkle cinnamon chips evenly over the triangles. Gently press the cinnamon chips into the dough and roll up. Place the rolls on an ungreased cookie sheet. Bake 10–12 minutes or until rolls are golden brown. Sprinkle with powdered sugar and cinnamon. Serve warm.

Zucchini BREAD

2 eggs
2 cups sugar
1 cup oil
1 tablespoon vanilla extract
2 cups zucchini, grated
1 teaspoon baking soda

1 teaspoon salt
3 cups flour
$\frac{1}{4}$ teaspoon baking powder
1 tablespoon cinnamon
$\frac{1}{2}$ cup chopped nuts
$\frac{1}{2}$ cup raisins

Preheat oven to 325°. Grease and flour two loaf pans; set aside. In a large bowl, add eggs, sugar, and oil. Beat with an electric hand mixer on low speed until well blended. Add vanilla and grated zucchini. Sift and add dry ingredients. Stir in nuts and raisins. Pour batter into prepared pans. Bake for 45–60 minutes or until toothpick inserted in center comes out clean.

Something made with

loving hands and

the finest ingredients

tastes best.

Cranberry NUT BREAD

2 cups all-purpose flour
¾ cup powdered sugar
¾ teaspoon salt
1½ teaspoons baking powder
½ teaspoon baking soda
1 cup cranberries, chopped
½ cup nuts, chopped
1 egg
2 tablespoons vegetable oil
¾ cup orange juice
1 tablespoon orange peel, grated

Preheat oven to 350°. Grease a 9x5-inch loaf pan. In a large bowl, combine the flour, sugar, salt, baking powder, and baking soda. Add the cranberries and nuts. Stir to coat with the flour. In a small bowl, combine the egg, oil, orange juice, and grated orange peel; stir. Add the egg mixture to the flour mixture and stir until combined. Pour the batter into the prepared pan. Bake for 50–60 minutes or until a toothpick inserted into the center comes out clean. Let cool for 10 minutes before removing from the pan and placing on a cooling rack. Cool for 60 minutes before slicing.

White FRUITCAKE

3 cups mixed candied fruit
2 cups gold raisins
1 ½ cups candied pineapple
1 ½ cups glazed cherries
1 ½ cups almonds, chopped
1 cup glazed mixed peel
2 cups flour
2 teaspoon baking powder

½ teaspoon salt
½ cup softened butter
1 cup sugar
3 eggs
1 tablespoon coarsely
    grated orange rind
1 teaspoon almond flavoring
½ cup orange juice

Line 2 loaf pans with greased waxed paper. Combine fruits and almonds. Toss with ½ cup of the flour and set aside. Mix dry ingredients and set aside. Cream butter and sugar until fluffy. Beat in eggs one at a time; add rind and flavoring, and beat again. Stir in flour mix alternately with juice until combined. Fold in fruit and pour into pans. Bake at 250° for 2 ½ hours with a pan of water or until done. Cool completely before removing from pans.

Strawberry BREAD

2 1/2 cups fresh strawberries
3 1/8 cups all-purpose flour
2 cups powdered sugar
1 tablespoon ground cinnamon
1 teaspoon salt

1 teaspoon baking soda
1 1/4 cups vegetable oil
4 eggs, beaten
1 1/4 cups chopped pecans

Preheat oven to 350°. Butter and flour two 9x5-inch loaf pans. Slice the strawberries and place them in a medium bowl. Sprinkle sugar lightly over them and set aside. Mix the flour, sugar, cinnamon, salt, and baking soda in a large bowl. Stir the oil and eggs into the bowl with the strawberries. Add the strawberry mixture to the flour mixture; stir well. Add the pecans; stir. Divide the batter and pour into the two prepared pans. Bake for 45–60 minutes, or until toothpick inserted in the center comes out clean. Let cool in pans for 10 minutes before turning loaves out. Cool completely on wire rack before slicing.

Jewelled FRUITCAKE

$^3/_4$ cup flour
$^3/_4$ cup sugar
$^1/_2$ teaspoon baking powder
$^1/_2$ teaspoon salt
3 eggs, beaten
$1^1/_2$ teaspoons vanilla
1 8-ounce package (2 cups) dried apricots
1 8-ounce package ($1^1/_2$ cups) pitted dates
1 cup drained green maraschino cherries
1 cup drained red maraschino cherries
1 cup candied pineapple, cut up
$^3/_4$ pound whole Brazil nuts

Mix dry ingredients with eggs and vanilla. Add fruit and nuts. Spread evenly in 2 loaf tins lined with greased aluminum foil. Bake at 275° for $1^3/_4$ hours or until toothpick comes out clean when you poke it. If necessary, cover with foil the last 30 minutes of cooking to prevent overbrowning. Remove from pans and cool. Wrap in plastic or aluminum foil. Store in cool place.

Cinnamon BREAD

2 cups flour
1 cup sugar
2 teaspoons baking powder
$\frac{1}{2}$ teaspoon baking soda
1 $\frac{1}{2}$ teaspoons ground
  cinnamon
1 teaspoon salt
1 cup buttermilk

$\frac{1}{4}$ cup vegetable oil
2 eggs
2 teaspoons vanilla
  extract
2 tablespoons sugar
1 teaspoon ground
  cinnamon
2 teaspoons margarine

Preheat oven to 350°. Grease a 9x5-inch loaf pan. In a large mixing bowl, combine flour, 1 cup sugar, baking powder, baking soda, 1$\frac{1}{2}$ teaspoons cinnamon, salt, buttermilk, oil, eggs, and vanilla. Beat with an electric hand mixer on low speed for 3 minutes. Pour mixture into the prepared loaf pan. Smooth the top with a spatula. In a small bowl, combine 2 tablespoons sugar, 1 teaspoon cinnamon, and margarine, stirring until crumbly. Sprinkle topping over smoothed batter. Using a knife, cut through the topping in a light swirling motion to give a marbled effect. Bake for 45–50 minutes, or until toothpick inserted in the center comes out clean. Allow to cool for 10 minutes before removing bread from pan. Allow to cool completely on wire rack before slicing.

Paradise LOAF

⅔ cup butter
1 cup sugar
3 eggs
3 cups flour
¼ teaspoon salt
1 teaspoon baking powder
½ cup milk
1 pound raisins
2 rings glazed pineapple, diced
½ cup glazed cherries, cut in half
1 teaspoon rum flavoring

Cream butter; add sugar and then the eggs one at a time, beating well. Sift dry ingredients and add to mixture alternately with milk. Blend the fruit together and fold into mixture, along with flavoring. Pour into greased loaf pan and bake at 325° for approximately 1 hour.

Peace on earth will come to stay,
When we live Christmas every day.

HELEN STEINER RICE

Norwegian HOLIDAY BREAD

1/2 cup butter
1/2 cup milk
1 package dry yeast
1/2 cup warm water
1/4 cup sugar
1 teaspoon salt
1 cup raisins

1/2 cup chopped candied
    cherries (red and
    green)
1/2 cup almonds
1 egg, slightly beaten
3 1/2–4 cups flour
Icing sugar

Heat butter and milk until butter is melted; cool to lukewarm. Soften yeast in warm water. Stir in sugar, salt, raisins, cherries, and nuts. Mix egg into cooled milk mixture. Add flour to form a stiff dough, beating well after each addition. Let rise in warm place until doubled in bulk, 1 1/2–2 hours. Turn on floured board. Toss lightly until coated with flour and not sticky. Divide dough into 2 parts and shape into round loaves. Place on greased baking sheets or 2 well-greased 8-inch round pans. Divide dough into 3 parts; shape dough into round loaves and place in 3 well-greased coffee tins. Let rise until doubled in bulk. Bake at 350° for 30–35 minutes. If desired, glaze with icing sugar mixed with just enough water to make a nice glaze.

Cherry POUND CAKE

¾ pound butter
1 ½ cups sugar
6 eggs
1 teaspoon vanilla
3 cups flour
½ teaspoon salt
1 teaspoon baking powder
1 cup candied cherries, halved

Cream butter and sugar; add beaten egg yolks and vanilla. Stir in dry ingredients with cherries. Gently fold in stiffly beaten egg whites. Bake at 325° for 1 hour 45 minutes.

Holiday PUMPKIN BREAD

1 (15-ounce) can solid-pack pumpkin
4 eggs
1 cup vegetable oil
²/₃ cup water
3 cups sugar
3 ¹/₂ cups all-purpose flour
2 teaspoons baking soda
1 ¹/₂ teaspoons salt
1 teaspoon ground cinnamon
1 teaspoon ground nutmeg
¹/₂ teaspoon ground cloves
¹/₄ teaspoon ground ginger

Preheat oven to 350°. Grease and flour two 9x5-inch loaf pans. In a medium bowl, combine pumpkin, eggs, oil, water, and sugar; mix until well blended. In a large bowl, whisk together the flour, baking soda, salt, cinnamon, nutmeg, cloves, and ginger. Add the dry ingredients to the pumpkin mixture and stir until blended. Pour into the prepared pans. Bake for 50–60 minutes or until toothpick inserted in the center comes out clean. Makes 2 loaves.

Christmas BREAD

1 loaf frozen white bread dough, thawed
1/2 cup mixed candied fruit
1/4 cup chopped or sliced almonds
Soft butter or margarine
2 tablespoons sugar
1/2 teaspoon cinnamon
Vanilla icing (optional)

Let dough rise until doubled in size. Roll out on floured surface into 14x7-inch rectangle. Sprinkle half with fruit and almonds. Fold uncovered dough over fruits; roll out again. Shape into round ball. Place into greased 9-inch round pan. Brush top with butter. Sprinkle cinnamon sugar mixture over top. Cover; let rise in warm place until doubled in size, about 1–1 1/2 hours. Bake at 350° until golden brown, about 30–35 minutes. Frost with vanilla icing and decorate with additional candied fruit and almond slices, if desired.

 Nut BREAD

4 cups flour
4 teaspoons baking powder
$\frac{1}{2}$ teaspoon salt
1 cup brown sugar
1 cup walnuts
1 egg
2 cups milk
1 teaspoon melted butter

Sift flour, baking powder, and salt together. Add brown sugar and nuts. Beat egg and mix with milk, then stir into dry mixture. Beat in melted butter and put into bread pan. Let rise for 20 minutes. Bake in 250° oven for 30 minutes or until golden.

*"Listen, listen to me,
and eat what is good,
and your soul will delight
in the richest of fare."*

ISAIAH 55:2

Banana POUND CAKE

1 package yellow cake mix
$1/3$ cup salad oil
$1 1/3$ cups mashed banana (approximately 3)
1 package instant vanilla pudding
4 eggs at room temperature
$1/2$ cup water
$1/2$ teaspoon cinnamon
$1/2$ teaspoon nutmeg
Confectioners' sugar

Combine all ingredients and beat for 4 minutes. Pour into 10-inch tube pan (greased) and bake for 1 hour at 325°. Dust with confectioners' sugar before serving.

Lemon LOAF

$^1/_2$ cup butter
1 cup sugar
2 eggs, well beaten
$^1/_2$ cup milk
Rind of 1 lemon

$^1/_4$ teaspoon salt
1 $^1/_2$ cups flour
1 teaspoon baking powder
1 $^1/_2$ cups glazed cherries,
    dredged in flour

Topping:

Juice of 1 lemon

$^1/_4$ cup sugar

Cream butter; add sugar and cream until light. Add eggs, mixing well. Add milk and stir. Add rind. Sift together salt, flour, and baking powder and add to mixture. Fold in cherries. Bake in an ungreased loaf pan at 350° for approximately 1 hour. Mix topping and pour over top of loaf while loaf is still hot.

Poppyseed LOAF

Batter:

¼ cup poppyseeds
¾ cup milk
½ cup butter or margarine
¾ cup sugar
2 eggs
1 teaspoon lemon juice

2 cups flour
2½ teaspoons baking powder
Pinch salt
½ cup maraschino cherries, well drained and halved

Glaze:

5 tablespoons brown sugar
2 tablespoons cream or milk
1 tablespoon butter or margarine
1–2 tablespoons crushed nuts

Put poppyseeds and milk in small bowl. Let stand for 30 minutes. Combine butter, sugar, and 1 egg in mixing bowl. Beat well. Add second egg and lemon juice. Beat until smooth. Stir in poppyseed mixture. Measure flour, baking powder, and salt together in small bowl. Mix well. Stir into batter until just moistened. Fold in cherries. Pour into greased loaf pan. Bake in 350° oven for 1 hour. Mix and pour glaze over top (optional).

Monkey BREAD

1 cup sugar
2 teaspoons ground cinnamon
3 (12-ounce) packages refrigerated
    biscuit dough
$\frac{1}{2}$ cup chopped walnuts (optional)
$\frac{1}{2}$ cup raisins (optional)
$\frac{1}{2}$ cup margarine
1 cup brown sugar, packed

Preheat oven to 350°. Grease a 9-inch tube pan. Combine sugar and cinnamon in a plastic bag. Cut biscuits into quarters. Shake 6–8 biscuit pieces at a time in the sugar-cinnamon mixture. Arrange the pieces in the bottom of the prepared pan. Continue until all biscuits are coated and placed in the pan. If using nuts and raisins, arrange them in the biscuit pieces as you go along. In a small saucepan, over medium heat, melt the margarine with the brown sugar. Boil for 1 minute. Pour the mixture over the biscuits. Bake for 35 minutes. Let bread cool in pan for 10 minutes, then turn the bread out onto a plate. Do not cut; pull bread apart.

Holiday BREAD TRAY

½ loaf banana nut bread, sliced
½ loaf pumpkin bread, sliced
½ loaf cranberry bread, sliced
½ loaf cinnamon bread, sliced
Butter or margarine
Cinnamon-flavored butter

Cut each slice of bread into 1-inch squares. Spread ⅓ of the bread squares with regular butter, ⅓ with cinnamon butter, and leave remaining squares plain. Place the bread squares on a holiday serving tray. Garnish with pieces of fruit and nuts if desired.

Cranberry Orange LOAF

$^1\!/_4$ cup butter or margarine
1 cup sugar
1 egg
Juice of 1 orange (water to make $^3\!/_4$ cup)
2 cups flour
$1\,^1\!/_2$ teaspoons baking powder
$^1\!/_2$ teaspoon baking soda
$^1\!/_2$ teaspoon salt
$1\,^1\!/_2$ cups frozen or fresh cranberries
Grated rind of 1 orange
$^1\!/_2$ cup chopped pecans or walnuts

Combine butter, sugar, and egg. Beat until smooth; stir in juice. Combine dry ingredients and fruit, rind, and nuts, and add to butter mixture, stirring just until moistened. Scrape into 9x5x3-inch loaf pan. Bake at 350° for 1 hour. Test with toothpick, but try not to poke cranberries. Let stand 10 minutes and remove from pan. Cool on rack; wrap and serve the next day.

Come, All Ye Shepherds

Come, all ye shepherds, ye children of earth,
Come ye, bring greetings to yon heavenly birth.
For Christ the Lord to all men is given,
To be our Savior sent down from heaven:
Come, welcome Him!

BOHEMIAN FOLK SONG

Cakes and Pies

You can never truly enjoy Christmas

until you can look up into

the Father's face and tell Him

you have received His Christmas gift.

JOHN R. RICE

FROZEN *Peppermint* CHEESECAKE

1 (8-ounce) package cream cheese, softened
1 (14-ounce) can sweetened
   condensed milk
1 cup hard peppermint candy, crushed
Red food coloring
2 cups frozen whipped topping, thawed
2 (9-inch) prepared chocolate crumb piecrusts

Place cream cheese in a large bowl. With an electric mixer on low speed, beat until fluffy. Gradually beat in sweetened condensed milk. Stir in crushed peppermint candy and food coloring. Fold in whipped topping. Pour into piecrusts and cover. Freeze 6 hours or until firm. Garnish with peppermint candies.

Queen Elizabeth CAKE

1 cup dates
1 cup hot water
1 teaspoon baking soda
1/4 cup butter
1 cup sugar
1 egg
1 1/2 cups flour
1 teaspoon baking powder

1/2 cup cream
1 teaspoon vanilla
6 teaspoons butter,
   melted
8 teaspoons brown sugar
4 teaspoons milk
1 cup shredded coconut

Cut up dates and pour hot water over dates with baking soda. Let cool. Mix 6 teaspoons butter, sugar, and egg, then add dry ingredients alternating with milk. Add dates and vanilla. Bake at 325° for 30 minutes. Beat together 1/4 cup butter, brown sugar, and milk. Mix in coconut. Spread on cake and put back in oven for another 10 minutes.

 Forest PIE

4 (1-ounce) baking chocolate squares, broken
into pieces
1 (14-ounce) can sweetened condensed milk
1 teaspoon almond extract
1 ½ cups frozen whipped topping, thawed
1 (9-inch) prepared piecrust
1 (21-ounce) can cherry pie filling, chilled

In a large saucepan, combine chocolate pieces and sweetened condensed milk. Cook over medium heat, stirring constantly, until chocolate is melted and smooth. Remove from heat and stir in almond extract. Pour mixture into a large bowl and allow to cool completely in the refrigerator. Beat cooled mixture until smooth. Fold the whipped topping into the chocolate mixture. Pour into the prepared piecrust. Refrigerate 4–5 hours or until set. Before serving, pour cherry pie filling over pie. Refrigerate leftover pie.

Cranberry Orange COFFEE CAKE

Crumb Topping:
- ³/₄ cup flour
- ½ cup margarine
- ½ cup sugar

Cream Cheese Layer:
- ½ pound cream cheese, softened
- ⅓ cup sugar
- 1 egg
- 1 teaspoon vanilla extract

Cake:
- 2 cups flour
- 1 cup sugar
- 1½ teaspoons baking powder
- ½ teaspoon baking soda
- ½ teaspoon salt
- ³/₄ cup orange juice
- ¼ cup margarine
- 1 teaspoon vanilla extract
- 1 egg, beaten
- 2 cups coarsely chopped fresh or frozen cranberries
- 2 tablespoons grated orange rind

Crumb Topping: Stir together and set aside.

Cream Cheese Layer: Beat cream cheese and sugar until light and fluffy. Beat in egg and vanilla; set aside.

Cake: Combine dry ingredients. Stir in juice, margarine, vanilla, and egg. Fold in cranberries and orange rind just until mixed. Pour into a 9-inch spring form pan. Spread cream cheese mixture over cake batter. Sprinkle with crumb topping. Bake at 350° for 65–70 minutes or until top springs back when lightly touched in center. Let cool on rack for 15 minutes. Remove outside ring and let cool completely. Makes 12 servings.

Apple CHEESECAKE

1 cup flour	½ cup sugar
½ cup butter	¼ teaspoon vanilla

Mix until crumbly and press into bottom of greased 9-inch spring form pan.

2 8-ounce packages	½ cup sugar
cream cheese	1 teaspoon vanilla
2 eggs	

Beat and pour over base.

4 cups sliced apples	5 teaspoons cinnamon
⅓ cup sugar	¼ cup chopped pecans
	or almonds

Shake apples in a bag with sugar and cinnamon. Divide evenly on top of cheesecake. Top with nuts. Chill.

Nehemiah said,
"Go and enjoy choice food and sweet drinks,
and send some to those
who have nothing prepared.
This day is sacred to our Lord.
Do not grieve,
for the joy of the LORD is your strength."

NEHEMIAH 8:10

 *Fruit Cocktail* CAKE

1 cup flour
1 cup sugar
1 teaspoon baking soda
$\frac{1}{2}$ teaspoon salt
1 egg
1 15-ounce can fruit cocktail, drained
$\frac{1}{2}$ cup brown sugar
$\frac{1}{2}$ cup coconut

Mix flour, sugar, soda, and salt. Add beaten egg and drained fruit cocktail. Pour into ungreased 8-inch square pan. Mix brown sugar and coconut and spread over top. Bake at 350° for 30–35 minutes.

Butterscotch PUDDING PIE

2 (3.9-ounce) packages instant butterscotch
    pudding mix
2 3/4 cups cold milk
1 (9-inch) prepared pie shell
1 cup frozen whipped topping, thawed

In a large bowl, combine the pudding mix and milk. Beat with a wire whisk for 2 1/2 minutes. Pour pudding into the prepared pie shell. Refrigerate for at least 1 hour or until the filling is set. Spoon whipped topping around the crust. Garnish the pie with holiday sprinkles scattered over the whipped topping. Keep refrigerated.

Orange CHEESECAKE

1 3-ounce package orange jelly powder
1 1/2 cups graham crumbs
1/4 cup butter
2 envelopes gelatin
1/2 cup cold water
1/2 cup milk
1 cup sugar
2 egg yolks
1 8-ounce package cream cheese
2 packages Dream Whip
2 egg whites
1 teaspoon vanilla
2 cans mandarin oranges, drained

Make jelly powder according to package directions; refrigerate until almost set. Combine crumbs and butter; press into 9x13-inch or free-form pan. Soak gelatin in 1/2 cup cold water; let stand. Combine milk, sugar, egg yolks, and mix well. Cook until thick, then add gelatin. Cool completely. Cream cheese until fluffy; add to gelatin mix. Beat Dream Whip, then beat egg whites until firm. Fold together, adding vanilla. Gently add drained orange pieces. Pour in pan over crust. Beat jelly until frothy; put on top. Refrigerate for 1 day before serving.

 CAKE

40 graham wafers, crushed
8 tablespoons butter
2 packages jelly powder, any flavor
1 cup hot water
1 cup sugar
Juice from 1 lemon
2 cans sweetened evaporated milk, chilled

Mix crumbs and butter; place 3 tablespoons aside for top. Spread balance over 9x12-inch pan. Dissolve jelly powder in hot water. Add sugar and lemon juice. Cool. Whip evaporated milk (which has been well chilled) until creamy. Add jelly powder mixture and beat until well mixed. Spread with remaining crumbs. Set in fridge.

The torch of love is

lit in the kitchen.

FRENCH PROVERB

STRAWBERRY  CAKE

1 small box strawberry-flavored gelatin
1 cup hot water
½ cup ice water
2 cups whipped topping, thawed
2 small cans frozen strawberries, drained
1 angel food cake
1 cup berry juice
1 tablespoon butter
1 tablespoon cornstarch

In a large bowl, combine gelatin, hot water, and ice water. Chill until slightly firm. Beat until stiff. Add whipped topping and drained strawberries. Break cake into pieces. Layer cake and gelatin mixture in 9x13-inch pan. End with cake on top. In a small saucepan, cook juice, butter, and cornstarch until clear. Cool. Drizzle over top of cake. Keep refrigerated.

 DESSERT CAKE—LEMON

1 angel food cake mix
1 pint vanilla ice cream
1 package lemon pie filling

Prepare cake mix as directed on package. Add 1 pint ice cream to hot lemon pie filling and whisk. Serve this sauce over slices of angel food cake and decorate with kiwi or other fruit.

Angel Food DESSERT CAKE—
PINEAPPLE

1 package instant vanilla pudding
1 tin crushed pineapple
1 pint whipping cream
1 angel food cake, cut into 3 layers

Add instant pudding to crushed pineapple (with juice) and let stand for 10 minutes. Whip the cream and add the pudding/pineapple mixture. Put a generous amount of filling between layers and continue to ice top and sides of cake. Keep the cake refrigerated.

Chocolate Chip CHEESECAKE

1 ½ cups finely crushed Oreo cookies
3 tablespoons butter, melted
3 small packages cream cheese, softened
1 can Eagle sweetened condensed milk
2 teaspoons vanilla
3 eggs
1 cup semisweet chocolate chips, divided
1 teaspoon flour

Combine Oreo crumbs and butter; press into 9-inch spring form pan. Beat cream cheese until fluffy, then beat in milk, vanilla, and eggs. Toss ½ cup chocolate chips with flour to coat; stir into cheese mixture. Pour into prepared pan and sprinkle with remaining chips. Bake for 1 hour at 300° or until cake springs back when lightly touched. Cool. Chill. Serve.

VERY *Berry* PIE

1 cup water
¾ cup sugar
2 tablespoons cornstarch
3 tablespoons raspberry-flavored gelatin
3¼ cups sliced strawberries

1 cup blueberries
1 cup raspberries
1 (9-inch) ready-to-use shortbread piecrust
Whipped topping (optional)

In a medium saucepan, over medium heat, combine water, sugar, and cornstarch. Bring to a boil, stirring constantly. Boil and stir for 1 minute; remove from heat. Add gelatin and stir until dissolved. Refrigerate about 30 minutes, stirring occasionally, until mixture thickens. Stir the berries into the gelatin mixture. Pour into the prepared crust. Refrigerate about 2 hours or until set. Top with whipped cream if desired. Store covered in the refrigerator.

Cookies and Cream PIE

1 (3.9-ounce) package instant chocolate pudding mix
1 (8-ounce) container frozen whipped topping, thawed
1 (9-inch) prepared chocolate crumb piecrust
1 ½ cups chocolate sandwich cookies, crushed

Prepare the pudding as directed on the package for pie filling; allow to set. When the pudding is ready, fold in the whipped topping. Add the crushed cookies; stir. Pour mixture into the prepared piecrust. Freeze pie until firm. Thaw in the refrigerator before serving.

Blueberry CHEESECAKE

2 cups graham crumbs
$\frac{1}{4}$ cup butter, melted
$\frac{1}{2}$ cup sugar
1 8-ounce package cream cheese, softened
2 packages Dream Whip
2 cups blueberries, fresh or frozen (patted dry)

Mix crumbs and butter; press into 13x9-inch pan. Sprinkle sugar on blueberries; set aside. Whip together cream cheese and Dream Whip (prepared according to directions on package). Gently stir in blueberries; pour into crust. Chill.

Worship the LORD your God,
and his blessing will be
on your food and water.

EXODUS 23:25

Cream Cheese APPLE CAKE

Pastry:

1 ¼ cups flour
⅓ cup sugar
½ cup margarine

1 egg yolk
¼ teaspoon vanilla

Mix flour with sugar. Cut in margarine. Beat egg yolk with vanilla. With fork, stir egg mixture into flour mixture. Press into bottom half-way up sides of a 9-inch spring form pan.

Topping:

4–5 apples (peeled, cored, quartered, and scored)
4 ounces cream cheese
¾ cup sugar

1 teaspoon vanilla
2 eggs
½ cup light cream
Nutmeg, to taste

Arrange apples on the pastry. Beat cream cheese until fluffy. Gradually beat sugar and vanilla. Add eggs one at a time, then light cream. Pour this mixture over the apples; sprinkle with nutmeg. Bake at 400° for 50–60 minutes. Serve warm or cool. Variation: Use blueberries instead of apples.

Chocolate CHEESECAKE

$\frac{1}{2}$ cup butter or margarine, melted
1 $\frac{1}{2}$ cups graham cracker crumbs
$\frac{1}{2}$ cup sugar
$\frac{2}{3}$ cup water
1 envelope gelatin, unflavored
2 (8-ounce) packages cream cheese, softened
4 (1-ounce) squares semisweet chocolate, melted
1 (14-ounce) can sweetened condensed milk
1 teaspoon vanilla extract
1 cup whipped cream

In a 9-inch springform pan, mix together the butter, graham cracker crumbs, and sugar. Press firmly against the bottom of the pan (do not line the sides). In a small saucepan, add $\frac{2}{3}$ cup water. Sprinkle the gelatin over the water and let stand for 1 minute. Over low heat, stir the gelatin until it dissolves; set aside. In a large bowl, beat the cream cheese and chocolate until fluffy. Gradually beat in the sweetened condensed milk. Add the vanilla and beat until smooth. Stir the gelatin mixture into the cream cheese mixture. Fold in the whipped cream. Pour the mixture into the prepared pan. Chill in the refrigerator for 3 hours or until set. Garnish with whipped cream. Keep refrigerated.

Cherry BUNDT CAKE

1 ¼ cups butter, softened
2 ¾ cups sugar
5 eggs
1 teaspoon almond extract
3 cups flour
1 teaspoon baking powder
¼ teaspoon salt
1 cup unsweetened evaporated milk
1 cup quartered maraschino cherries,
    well drained
Sifted icing sugar

Beat butter, sugar, eggs, and extract in large bowl on low speed of electric mixer until blended, then on high speed 5 minutes until light and fluffy. Combine flour, baking powder, and salt. Add dry ingredients alternately with evaporated milk to creamed mixture, mixing lightly after each addition. Fold in cherries. Turn batter into greased 12-cup Bundt or tube pan. Bake at 350° for 75–85 minutes. Cover with foil for last 10 minutes if becoming too brown. Cool in pan 10 minutes. Remove from pan. Cool completely. Dust with icing sugar before serving. A white icing drizzle is a pretty alternative decoration.

Pineapple Dream CAKE

36 large marshmallows
1 cup milk
1 pint whipping cream
1 cup drained crushed pineapple
15 graham wafers

Melt marshmallows in milk. Whip cream, then fold in pineapple. Crush wafers and cover bottom of 9x9-inch pan (save some for sprinkling). Add marshmallow mixture to pineapple mixture. Pour into pan. Sprinkle remaining crushed wafers on top. Chill.

Magic Cherry CHIFFON CHEESECAKE

1 unbaked 9-inch pie shell (or 1 9-inch graham
    cracker crumb crust
1 small package cream cheese, softened
½ can Eagle Brand sweetened condensed milk
2 eggs, separated
2 tablespoons lemon juice
Pinch salt
1 can cherry pie filling

Bake pie shell according to package instructions. While crust is cooling,
prepare filling. Beat cream cheese until fluffy. Add condensed milk and
egg yolks and beat until smooth. Stir in lemon juice. Beat egg whites
with salt to soft peaks. Fold into mixture. Pour into baked pie shell.
Bake at 300° for 30 minutes or until cake springs back when lightly
touched. Chill and top with cherry pie filling. For a variation: top with
blueberry pie filling.

Honey CAKE

1 cup brown sugar
5 eggs
1 cup creamed honey
1 cup oil
1 cup sour cream
2¾–3 cups flour
1¼ teaspoons baking powder
1¼ teaspoons baking soda

Beat sugar and eggs; add honey and beat well. Add oil slowly, beating on lower speed until thoroughly blended. Add sour cream and beat. Combine flour, baking powder, and soda and add to mixture. Beat slowly until smooth. Pour into greased 9x12-inch pan. Bake for approximately 1 hour in a 350° oven.

*As honey is
sweet and pleasant to the taste,
so wisdom is to the soul.*

SEE PROVERBS 24:13–14

Raisin AND Rhubarb PIE

1 cup rhubarb, fresh or frozen
1 cup raisins
1 cup sugar
1 lemon, juice and grated rind
1 egg
1 premade crust, fresh or frozen

If rhubarb is fresh, peel and cut into ½-inch pieces. Cover with boiling water; let stand 5 minutes and drain. Wash raisins and mix with rhubarb. Add other ingredients. Pour into pie shell. Bake 30–35 minutes at 325° or until golden brown.

Pretzel CHEESECAKE

1 cup pretzel crumbs
$\frac{1}{4}$ cup butter, melted
$\frac{1}{2}$ cup sugar
1 container frozen whipped topping, thawed
1 (3-ounce) package cream cheese, softened
$\frac{1}{2}$ cup powdered sugar
1 (21-ounce) can cherry pie filling

In a 9-inch pie pan, combine pretzel crumbs, butter, and sugar. Press into bottom of pan to form a crust; set aside. Combine whipped topping, cream cheese, and powdered sugar in a medium bowl; beat well. Spread filling over prepared crust. Top with cherry pie filling. Chill in refrigerator for at least 2 hours before serving.

CREAMY *Lime* PIE

1 (14-ounce) can sweetened condensed milk
$\frac{1}{2}$ cup lime juice (from concentrate)
Green food coloring
1 cup whipped cream
1 (9-inch) prepared graham cracker piecrust
Whipped cream (optional)
Lime slices (optional)

In a large bowl, combine sweetened condensed milk, lime juice, and green food coloring; stir well. Fold in the whipped cream. Pour the mixture into the prepared piecrust. Chill pie in the refrigerator for 3 hours or until filling is set. Garnish with whipped cream and lime slices if desired. Keep refrigerated.

 Macaroon CAKE

Cake:

¹/₂ cup butter	1 cup flour
¹/₂ cup sugar	2 teaspoons baking powder
4 egg yolks	2 tablespoons milk

Cream butter and sugar; add egg yolks and beat. Sift flour and baking powder and add alternately with milk. Pour into 9x9-inch pan.

Meringue:

4 egg whites	¹/₂ cup sugar
Pinch of salt	1 cup coconut (unsweetened)

Beat egg whites with salt until peaks form. Add sugar and continue beating. Fold in coconut and spread on base. Bake at 325° for approximately 40 minutes.

Pistachio CHEESECAKE

For variation, try using chocolate pudding.

Base:

½ cup butter or margarine   1 cup flour
3 tablespoons icing sugar

Mix together; press into an 8x13-inch pan. Bake at 325° for 15–20 minutes; cool.

Filling:

⅔ cup icing sugar   1 8-ounce package cream
½ tub large Cool Whip   cheese, softened

Whip and spread on cooled base.

Topping:

2 packages pistachio (or chocolate) instant pudding
2½ cups milk

Whip until slightly thick; pour over filling. Top with other half Cool Whip and refrigerate.

Chocolate DREAM PIE

2 envelopes Dream Whip
1 ³/₄ cups milk
2 packages chocolate instant pudding
  (4-serving size)
1 9-inch pie shell, baked and cooled (or 1 9-inch
  graham cracker crumb crust)

Prepare dessert topping mix as directed on package, using large mixer bowl. Add milk and pudding mix. Blend, then beat on high speed for 2 minutes, scraping bowl occasionally. Spoon into pie shell. Chill for 3 hours.

Cherry CHEESE PIE

1 (8-ounce) package cream cheese, softened
$\frac{1}{2}$ cup sugar
2 cups frozen whipped topping, thawed
1 (9-inch) prepared graham cracker crust
1 (21-ounce) can cherry pie filling

In a medium bowl, beat together cream cheese and sugar until fluffy. Fold in whipped topping and stir until the mixture is smooth. Pour into the prepared graham cracker crust. Cover and refrigerate for 3 hours. Spoon the cherry pie filling over top of the pie. Keep refrigerated.

*"Who then is
the faithful and wise servant,
whom the master has put in charge of
the servants in his household
to give them their food
at the proper time?"*

MATTHEW 24:45

 Coffee CAKE

Topping:

        1/3 cup brown sugar   1/4 cup walnuts

        1/3 cup sugar   1–1 1/2 teaspoons cinnamon

Cake:

        1/2 cup butter   1 1/4 cups sour cream

        1 cup sugar   2 cups flour

        2 eggs, beaten   2 teaspoons baking powder

        1 teaspoon vanilla   1 teaspoon baking soda

Mix topping ingredients and set aside. Cream butter and sugar; add eggs and vanilla, then sour cream. Mix in dry ingredients. Place half of batter in a well-greased pan, then sprinkle on half the topping. Pour in remaining batter; top with rest of topping. Bake at 350° for 35–45 minutes.

Grasshopper PIE

1 (8-ounce) package cream cheese, softened
1 (14-ounce) can sweetened condensed milk
Green food coloring
16 chocolate mint cookies, crushed
1 (8-ounce) container frozen whipped topping, thawed
1 (9-inch) prepared chocolate crumb piecrust

Place cream cheese in a large bowl. Beat with an electric mixer, on low speed, until fluffy. Gradually beat in the sweetened condensed milk until smooth. Add the food coloring; stir. Stir in the crushed cookies, saving some for garnish. Fold in the whipped topping. Pour the mixture into the prepared piecrust. Chill in the refrigerator for 3 hours or until filling is set. Garnish with cookie pieces. Keep refrigerated.

No-Bake PUMPKIN PIE

4 ounces cream cheese, softened
1 tablespoon milk
1 tablespoon sugar
1 1/2 cups frozen whipped topping, thawed
1 (9-inch) prepared graham cracker piecrust
1 cup cold milk
2 (3.9-ounce) packages instant vanilla
    pudding mix
1 (15-ounce) can pumpkin puree
1 teaspoon ground cinnamon
1/2 teaspoon ground ginger
1/4 teaspoon ground cloves
Additional whipped topping, thawed

In a large bowl, whisk together the cream cheese, milk, and sugar until mixture is smooth. Fold in the whipped topping; stir well. Spread mixture onto the bottom of prepared crust. In a large bowl, combine milk, pudding mix, pumpkin, cinnamon, ginger, and cloves; mix well. When the pudding mixture is thick, spread it over the cream cheese layer. Refrigerate for 4 hours or until set. Garnish with whipped topping. Keep refrigerated.

Fudge Ribbon CAKE

2 tablespoons butter
1 8-ounce package
    cream cheese
2 1/4 cups sugar
1 tablespoon cornstarch
3 eggs
1 1/3 cups plus 2 tablespoons
    milk
1 1/2 teaspoons vanilla

2 cups flour
1 teaspoon salt
1 teaspoon baking
    powder
1/2 teaspoon baking
    soda
1/2 cup butter, room
    temperature
3 squares unsweetened
    chocolate

Cream 2 tablespoons butter with cream cheese; add 1/4 cup sugar and cornstarch. Add 1 egg and 2 tablespoons sugar. Then add 1 egg, 2 tablespoons milk, and 1/2 teaspoon vanilla. Beat at high speed until smooth and creamy. Set aside. Grease and flour bottom of 13x9-inch pan. Combine flour with 2 cups sugar, salt, baking powder, and soda in large mixing bowl. Add 1/2 cup butter and 1 cup milk. Blend well at low speed. Add 1/3 cup milk, 2 eggs, chocolate, and 1 teaspoon vanilla, and continue beating 1 1/2 minutes at low speed. Spread half of batter in pan. Spoon cheese mixture over batter. Top with remaining batter. Bake at 350° for 50–60 minutes. Cool and frost if desired.

CHOCOLATE *Turtle* CHEESECAKE

1 (7-ounce) package caramels
¼ cup evaporated milk
¾ cup chopped pecans, divided
1 (9-inch) prepared chocolate crumb piecrust
2 (3-ounce) packages cream cheese, softened
½ cup sour cream
1¼ cups milk
1 (3.9-ounce) package instant chocolate
   pudding mix
½ cup fudge topping

Place caramels and evaporated milk in a large saucepan. Mix over medium heat, stirring constantly until smooth. Stir in ½ cup chopped pecans. Pour into the piecrust. Combine cream cheese, sour cream, milk, and pudding mix in a blender. Process until smooth. Pour pudding mixture over caramel layer, covering evenly. Loosely cover pie and chill until set. Drizzle fudge topping over pudding layer in a decorative pattern. Sprinkle top of cake with remaining pecans. Loosely cover and chill in refrigerator.

 LAYERED JELLY CAKE

2 cups graham crumbs
1/3 cup butter or margarine
2 packages red jelly powder
1 small can evaporated milk
3 packages green jelly powder
2 packages orange jelly powder

2 packages blue (or dark color) jelly powder
1/2 cup cold milk
1/2 teaspoon vanilla
1 package Dream Whip

Bottom: Mix crumbs and butter; press into 9x13-inch pan.

1st layer: Mix 2 red jelly powders with 1 cup boiling water; add 2 cups cold water. When partially set, whip evaporated milk and beat with jelly powder. Pour over bottom.

2nd layer: Mix 3 packages green jelly powder with 1 cup boiling water; add 2 cups cold water. When almost set, pour over first layer.

3rd layer: Mix 2 packages orange jelly powder with 1 cup boiling water; add 1 cup cold water. When almost set, whip until fluffy (just whipped jelly powder, no extras). Pour over second layer.

4th layer: Mix 2 packages blue jelly powder with 1/2 cup boiling water. Set until firm; slice into squares. Using milk and vanilla, mix Dream Whip according to package instructions; fold in jelly powder squares, then spread over third layer.

*"He will provide
delicacies fit for a king."*

GENESIS 49:20

Blueberry CREAM PIE

2 cups milk
1 tablespoon butter
2 tablespoons lemon juice, divided
1 teaspoon vanilla
2 eggs, beaten
1/4 cup hot water
3/4 cup sugar, divided
2 cups blueberries, drained if frozen
4 1/2 tablespoons cornstarch
1 baked pie shell, cooled
1 pint whipping cream, whipped

Heat milk gently; add butter, 1 tablespoon lemon juice, and 1 teaspoon vanilla. Bring to boil then add beaten eggs; boil until thickened. Cool and pour into pie shell. Add 1 tablespoon lemon juice, water, and 1/4 cup sugar to blueberries. Bring to a boil and thicken with 1 1/2 tablespoons cornstarch mixed in just enough water so it doesn't make lumps when added to blueberry mixture. Cool; pour on top of pie. Top with whipped cream. Garnish with a few leftover blueberries.

Chocolate PIE

3 (1-ounce) squares semisweet
  chocolate
1 (14-ounce) can sweetened
  condensed milk
¼ teaspoon salt
¼ cup hot water

2 egg yolks
1 teaspoon vanilla extract
1 cup whipped cream
1 (9-inch) prepared pie shell
Additional whipped cream
Chocolate shavings

In a large saucepan, combine chocolate, sweetened condensed milk, and salt. Cook over medium heat until thick and bubbly, stirring constantly. Add water and egg yolks, stirring quickly until the mixture is thick and bubbly again. Remove from heat and stir in the vanilla. Allow to cool for 15 minutes. Chill in the refrigerator for an additional 20–30 minutes; stir. Fold the whipped cream into the cooled chocolate mixture; stir. Pour the chocolate mixture into the prepared pie shell. Chill for 2½–3 hours, or until chocolate is set. Top with the additional whipped cream. Garnish with chocolate shavings. Keep refrigerated.

*Perfect* LEMON PIE

Filling:

7 tablespoons cornstarch
1 ½ cups sugar
½ teaspoon salt
2 cups boiling water
3 egg yolks

¼ cup lemon juice
2 tablespoons butter
2 tablespoons grated
    lemon peel
1 baked pastry shell

Meringue:

3 egg whites
6 tablespoons sugar

Pinch cream of tartar
Pinch salt

Combine cornstarch, sugar, and salt. Add water. Cook until thick, stirring constantly. Beat egg yolks slightly. Add a little hot water mixture; stir and pour all back into main mixture. Cook 2 minutes, stirring constantly. Remove from heat and stir in lemon juice, butter, and lemon rind. Cool to room temperature without stirring. Pour into pastry shell. To make meringue, beat 3 egg whites until it makes fine foam mounds. Add 6 tablespoons sugar, 1 tablespoon at a time. Beat after each addition; at last addition, add cream of tartar and salt. Beat until consistency is right. Spread on filling, and bake at 350° for 15 minutes or until slightly golden.

Raspberry Rainbow CAKE

1 package (2-layer size) white cake mix
1 single package raspberry jelly powder
1 tub Cool Whip

Prepare cake mix as directed on package using a well-greased and floured 13x9-inch pan and bake at 350° for 35 minutes. Cool in pan 15 minutes. Poke with fork at $\frac{1}{2}$-inch intervals. (Do not remove from pan.) Prepare jelly powder as directed on package and pour over cake in pan. Chill 4 hours. Garnish with Cool Whip.

ANY *Fruit* OR *Berry* PIE

Fruit or berries, fresh or frozen (enough to fill
   the pie shell)
3/4 cup sugar
2 cups water
2 tablespoons cornstarch
Pinch salt
1 small package jelly powder, same flavor as
   the fruit
1 baked pie shell, cooled
1 small container whipped cream

Drain berries, pat dry, and sprinkle with sugar. Set aside. Mix
water, cornstarch, and salt. Bring to a boil; add jelly powder and
mix until dissolved. Continue to boil until syrupy. Remove from
heat and let cool until the right consistency to add the fruit or
berries, partially set enough to mix smoothly and not have the
fruit sink. It also must be cool enough so as not to cook the fruit
or berries. Pour into baked pie shell. Chill completely. Top with
whipped cream. Serve.

Banana Butterscotch PIE

2 cups milk
1/3 cup flour
3/4 cup brown sugar
1/2 teaspoon salt
3 egg yolks, beaten

2 tablespoons butter
1/2 teaspoon vanilla
1 baked pie shell, cooled
2 large bananas
Sweetened whipped cream

Heat milk slowly in double boiler or microwave. Combine with dry ingredients and cook until thick, stirring frequently with a whisk. Stir small amount into beaten egg yolks, return to main mixture, and continue cooking 2 minutes longer. Remove from heat and beat in butter and vanilla. Cool slightly. Pour small amount over bottom of pie shell. Slice one banana over top. Pour in remaining filling. Chill. Serve with whipped cream and garnish with bananas.

Crunchy ICE CREAM CAKE

4 cups toasted rice cereal
  squares, crumbled
1/3 cup brown sugar
6 tablespoons butter, melted
1 (3.9-ounce) package instant
  butterscotch pudding mix

1/2 cup chunky peanut butter
1 2/3 cups milk
1 quart vanilla ice cream,
  softened
1/2 cup chopped peanuts

Grease a 9-inch square baking pan; set aside. In a large bowl, combine crumbled cereal, brown sugar, and butter; mix well. Measure 1/4 cup of the cereal mixture and set aside. Pat remaining cereal mixture firmly into the bottom of prepared pan. Refrigerate for about 1 hour or until firm. Using an electric mixer, combine butterscotch pudding mix, peanut butter, and milk on low speed until well blended; fold in vanilla ice cream and mix well. Pour ice cream mixture into prepared pan; sprinkle with reserved crumb mixture; then sprinkle with peanuts. Cover with aluminum foil and freeze at least 6 hours.

The cheerful heart has a continual feast.

PROVERBS 15:15

Pecan PIE

1 shell of your favorite pastry,
   uncooked
1 cup pecans
3 eggs
$\frac{1}{2}$ cup sugar
1 cup corn syrup
$\frac{1}{8}$ teaspoon salt
1 teaspoon vanilla
$\frac{1}{4}$ cup butter, melted

Line pie plate with pastry. Spread pecans on top. Set aside. Beat eggs; add sugar, syrup, salt, vanilla, and melted butter. Pour over top of pecans. Bake at 350° for 50–60 minutes.

French Apple PIE (TORTE)

Base:

1 ⅓ cups flour
3 tablespoons icing sugar

⅔ cup butter at room
   temperature

Filling:

¾ cup sugar
¼ teaspoon salt
2 tablespoons flour
½ teaspoon cinnamon

2 tablespoons butter at room
   temperature
7 thinly sliced apples

Topping:

1 ¼ cups flour
½ cup packed brown sugar

⅓ cup butter, room
   temperature

For pastry combine flour and icing sugar; cut in butter until crumbly. Press dough over bottom and 2 inches up sides of 9-inch spring form pan. Chill.

For filling combine dry ingredients and cut in butter. Add apples; toss to coat. Place apple mix in prepared crust.

For topping combine flour and brown sugar in bowl. Cut in butter. Squeeze handfuls of topping into firm chunks; break chunks apart into smaller pieces. Sprinkle over apples.

Bake at 350° for 60–75 minutes or until apples are done. Cover loosely with foil if browning too quickly. Cool completely.

Chocolate Ripple ORANGE CAKE

1 cup soft butter or margarine	1 teaspoon baking powder
1 cup sugar	1 teaspoon baking soda
3 large eggs	1 whole grated orange rind
1 cup sour cream	
1 ¾ cups flour	

Cream butter and sugar until light and fluffy. Add eggs; beat 1 minute at low speed. Blend in sour cream. Add dry ingredients and rind and blend thoroughly. Spoon ¼ cake batter into greased and floured 10-inch tube pan.

Alternate layers with:

½ cup sugar	1 heaping tablespoon cocoa
3 tablespoons cinnamon	

Bake at 325° for 60 minutes. Cool 10 minutes and invert.

While cooling, mix:

¼ cup orange juice	⅓ cup icing sugar

Boil for a few minutes and drizzle over cake.

Chocolate PEANUT BUTTER PIE

2 (3.9-ounce) packages single-serve, ready-
    made chocolate pudding
$^1/_3$ cup peanut butter
1 (8-ounce) container frozen whipped
    topping, thawed
1 (9-inch) prepared graham cracker crust

In a large bowl, combine the pudding and peanut butter. Stir
until mixture is smooth. Fold in the whipped topping and mix
until well blended. Pour the mixture into the prepared piecrust. Put pie in freezer until firm. Partially thaw in the refrigerator for about 2 hours before serving. Store in the freezer and
thaw as needed.

Pumpkin ICE CREAM PIE

1 ½ cups gingersnap crumbs
⅓ cup sugar
⅓ cup melted butter
1 envelope unflavored gelatin
¼ cup cold water
¾ cup canned pumpkin

¾ teaspoon salt
2 ¼ teaspoons pumpkin pie spice
1 ½ teaspoons vanilla
6 cups vanilla ice cream, softened
Prepared pie shell

Combine gingersnap crumbs, sugar, and butter; mix well. Press into a 9-inch pie plate. Refrigerate until needed. In a saucepan, soften gelatin in cold water. Stir in pumpkin, salt, and pie spice. Stir over low heat until gelatin is dissolved. Add vanilla and cool to room temperature. Fold ice cream into mixture. Pour into prepared pie shell. If desired, sprinkle with additional gingersnap crumbs. Freeze until firm. Remove from freezer 10 minutes before serving.

*"Give, and it will be given to you.
A good measure, pressed down,
shaken together and running over,
will be poured into your lap."*

LUKE 6:38

Candy and Fudge

*Be joyful in hope,
patient in affliction, faithful in prayer.
Share with God's people who are in need.
Practice hospitality.*

ROMANS 12:12–13

Butterscotch Fudge CUTOUTS

3⅓ cups butterscotch chips
1 (14-ounce) can sweetened condensed milk

Line a 15x10x1-inch jelly roll pan with aluminum foil. Combine butter-scotch chips and sweetened condensed milk in a large, microwave-safe bowl. Microwave on high (100%) for 1 minute. Continue heating for 15–20 seconds at a time, until the chips are melted and the mixture is smooth when stirred. Immediately spread into prepared pan. Cover and refrigerate until fudge is firm. Use the edges of the foil to lift fudge out of the pan. Peel off the foil and place fudge on a cutting board. Using small cookie cutters, cut fudge into shapes. Makes about 2 pounds.

Chocolate PEANUT CLUSTERS

2 tablespoons creamy peanut butter
1 (6-ounce) package semisweet
   chocolate chips
1 (6-ounce) package
   butterscotch chips
2 cups salted peanuts

In a medium saucepan, add peanut butter, chocolate chips, and butterscotch chips. Cook over medium heat until chips are melted and smooth. Remove from heat and add peanuts. Drop by rounded spoonfuls onto waxed paper.

Martha Washington CANDIES

1 cup margarine
4 cups powdered sugar
1 (14-ounce) can sweetened condensed milk
2 cups shredded coconut
2 cups chopped pecans
2 teaspoons vanilla extract
2 cups semisweet chocolate chips

Line two cookie sheets with waxed paper; set aside. In a large bowl, combine margarine, powdered sugar, and sweetened condensed milk; mix well. Add coconut, pecans, and vanilla. Mix until well combined. Chill until firm enough to handle. Form mixture into small balls and place on prepared cookie sheets. Chill until completely firm. Melt chocolate chips in a saucepan. Using a toothpick, dip the balls into the melted chocolate. Allow to cool on waxed paper.

Holiday PEANUT BUTTER CHOCOLATE FUDGE

3 cups (1 ½ packages) semisweet chocolate chips
1 (14-ounce) can sweetened condensed milk
Dash salt
½ cup chopped nuts (optional)
1 ½ teaspoons vanilla extract
1 ⅔ cups (10-ounce package) peanut butter chips, divided
½ cup whipping cream

Line an 8-inch square pan with waxed paper. Melt chocolate chips and sweetened condensed milk in a medium saucepan over low heat, stirring constantly. Stir in salt. Remove from heat. Stir in nuts, if desired, vanilla, and ⅔ cup peanut butter chips. Pour into prepared pan and spread evenly with a spatula. Melt the remaining peanut butter chips with the whipping cream over low heat, stirring constantly, until smooth and thick. Spread over chocolate. Refrigerate until firm. Turn the fudge onto a cutting board and peel off the waxed paper. Cut the fudge into squares. Store in an airtight container in the refrigerator.

*"The Lord Jesus himself said:
'It is more blessed to give
than to receive.'"*

ACTS 20:35

Chocolate-Covered CHERRIES

2 1/2 cups sugar
1/4 cup margarine
1 tablespoon milk
1/2 teaspoon almond extract
4 (4-ounce) jars maraschino cherries with stems,
    drained
2 cups semisweet chocolate chips
2 tablespoons shortening

In a medium bowl, combine sugar, margarine, milk, and almond extract; stir. On a lightly floured surface, knead the mixture into a large ball. Roll into 1-inch individual balls. Flatten the balls into 2-inch circles. Leaving the stems sticking out, wrap the cherries in the circles by lightly rolling in hands. Place the wrapped cherries on a sheet of waxed paper and chill in the refrigerator for at least 4 hours. In a medium saucepan over medium heat, melt the chocolate chips and shortening. Holding the balls by the stem of the cherry sticking out, dip the chilled cherries into the chocolate mixture. Chill in the refrigerator.

Pumpkin FUDGE

3 cups sugar
$^{3}/_{4}$ cup butter
$^{2}/_{3}$ cup evaporated milk
$^{1}/_{2}$ cup canned pumpkin
$^{1}/_{2}$ teaspoon ground cinnamon
$^{1}/_{4}$ teaspoon ground ginger
$^{1}/_{4}$ teaspoon ground nutmeg
1 (12-ounce) package butterscotch chips
1 (7-ounce) jar marshmallow crème
1 cup chopped pecans
1 teaspoon vanilla extract

Grease a 9x13-inch baking pan. In a large saucepan, combine the sugar, butter, evaporated milk, pumpkin, cinnamon, ginger, and nutmeg. Bring the mixture to a boil, stirring constantly. Reduce heat. Boil over medium heat until mixture registers 234° on a candy thermometer (about 25 minutes), stirring constantly. Remove from the heat and stir in the butterscotch chips until completely melted. Add the marshmallow crème, pecans, and vanilla. Mix until combined. Pour the mixture into the prepared pan. Spread evenly. Allow to cool at room temperature. Cut into squares and wrap tightly in plastic wrap. Store in the refrigerator.

Almond ROCA

1 tablespoon corn syrup
$^1/_4$ cup sugar
1 cup butter
$^1/_4$ cup water
1 $^1/_4$ cups toasted slivered almonds
1 6-ounce package chocolate chips

In a large, heavy saucepan, gently boil syrup, sugar, butter, and water until it reaches the "hard crack" stage on candy thermometer (300° F/150° C). Do not stir! This takes about 10 minutes. To be sure, drop a small amount of the mixture into cold water to see if it turns brittle. Remove from heat and add almonds. Spread onto an ungreased cookie sheet. Sprinkle with chocolate chips while still hot and spread evenly when melted. Cool in fridge or freezer. Break into bite-sized pieces. Note: This recipe does not double.

Chocolate-Covered PRETZELS

1 cup semisweet chocolate chips
1 cup white chocolate chips, divided
1½ tablespoons shortening, divided
25 small pretzels

Cover a cookie sheet with waxed paper. Combine chocolate chips, ⅔ cup white chocolate chips, and 1 tablespoon shortening in a large microwave-safe bowl. Microwave on high (100%) for 1 minute; stir. Microwave on high an additional 1–1½ minutes until chips are melted when stirred. Dip each pretzel into the mixture and place on the prepared cookie sheet. Combine the remaining ⅓ cup white chocolate chips and the ½ teaspoon shortening in a small microwave-safe bowl. Microwave on high for 20–30 seconds; stir. Using a toothpick, drizzle the mixture across the pretzels. Refrigerate until set. Store in an airtight container.

Easy Microwave PEANUT BRITTLE

1 cup sugar
½ cup light corn syrup
1 dash salt
1 cup shelled raw peanuts
1 tablespoon butter or margarine
1 teaspoon vanilla
1 ½ teaspoons baking soda

Grease a cookie sheet generously. Combine sugar, corn syrup, and salt in a 3-quart casserole dish; stir in the peanuts. Microwave on high (100%) for 8–10 minutes or until light brown. Stir in the remaining ingredients until the mixture is light and foamy. Quickly spread the mixture as thinly as possible on the prepared cookie sheet.

Peppermint PRETZEL CANES

6 ounces vanilla flavor candy coating, cut into pieces
2 tablespoons shortening
2/3 cup peppermint candies, finely crushed
12 pretzel rods

Line a cookie sheet with waxed paper. Melt candy coating and shortening in a medium saucepan over low heat, stirring occasionally. Pour the mixture into a shallow baking pan; carefully set the baking dish in hot water to keep the coating soft. Sprinkle the crushed peppermint candy over a separate sheet of waxed paper. Roll the pretzels in the hot coating, allowing excess to drip off. Roll each coated pretzel in crushed candy. Place on lined cookie sheet and let stand until set.

THE HISTORY OF THE *Candy Cane*

The candy cane, seen mostly during the holiday season, stands as an important Christmas symbol. A candy maker wanted to create a way to express the meaning of Christmas through the imagination of candy. That is when he came up with the idea of the candy cane. There are several different symbols incorporated into the candy cane. First, he used a plain white peppermint stick. The color white symbolizes the purity and sinless nature of Jesus. He then decided to add three red stripes to symbolize the pain inflicted upon Jesus before His death on the cross and a bold stripe to represent the blood He shed for mankind. He made it in the shape of a cane, so when looked at, it looks like a shepherd's staff, which represents that Jesus is the Shepherd of man. If you turn the cane upside down, you will notice the shape of the letter "J" symbolizing the first letter in Jesus' name. The candy cane serves as a lasting reminder of what Christmas is really all about.

Candy Cane BARK

8 ounces white chocolate
8 ounces dark chocolate
4 tablespoons candy canes, crushed

Place the white and dark chocolate in a microwave-safe bowl. Microwave on high (100%) for 30 seconds; stir. Continue microwaving at 30-second intervals until smooth when stirred. Add in crushed candy canes. Pour the mixture onto a cookie sheet in a thin layer. Freeze for up to 30 minutes. Break into small pieces.

Chocolate Butterscotch FUDGE

1 cup butterscotch chips
1 (14-ounce) can sweetened condensed milk
2 cups (12-ounce package) semisweet chocolate chips
1 teaspoon vanilla extract
$\frac{1}{2}$ cup chopped walnuts

Line an 8-inch square pan with aluminum foil. Combine butterscotch chips and $\frac{1}{3}$ cup sweetened condensed milk in a small microwave-safe bowl; set aside. Place chocolate chips, the remaining sweetened condensed milk, and vanilla in a medium, microwave-safe bowl. Microwave on high (100%) for 1 minute. Stir until the chips are completely melted. Stir in the walnuts. Spread evenly into the prepared pan. Microwave butterscotch chip mixture on high for 45 seconds. Stir until chips are completely melted. Spread evenly over the chocolate layer. Refrigerate until firm. Remove from the pan and peel off the foil. Place on a cutting board and cut into squares. Store in an airtight container in the refrigerator.

Peanut Butter

CHOCOLATE CHIP FUDGE

1 ½ cups sugar
⅔ cup (5-ounce can) evaporated milk
2 tablespoons butter
1 ½ cups miniature marshmallows
1 ¾ cups (11-ounce package) peanut butter
     and milk chocolate chips
1 teaspoon vanilla extract

Line an 8-inch square baking pan with aluminum foil. Grease foil with butter and set aside. Combine the sugar, evaporated milk, and butter in a large saucepan. Cook over medium heat, stirring constantly. Bring to a rolling boil. Boil, stirring constantly for 5 minutes. Remove from heat and stir in the marshmallows, chips, and vanilla. Continue stirring until marshmallows are completely melted. Pour mixture into prepared pan. Refrigerate for 1 hour or until firm. Cut fudge into squares. Store in an airtight container in a cool, dry place.

Coconut Almond BALLS

4 cups flaked coconut
¼ cup light corn syrup
¼ cup shortening
1 (12 ounce) package semisweet
  chocolate chips
26 whole almonds

Line two cookie sheets with waxed paper and place large cooling rack on top. Place the coconut in large bowl. Heat the corn syrup for 1 minute in the microwave or until syrup boils. Pour syrup immediately over coconut and stir until well mixed. Shape coconut into 26 balls and place on wire racks. Allow to set for 10 minutes, and then reroll each ball to keep loose ends from sticking out. Melt the shortening and chocolate chips together in large glass bowl in the microwave. Working quickly, spoon 1 tablespoon of the chocolate mixture over each ball. Lightly press an almond on top of each ball. Let stand until balls are set.

Five-minute NEVER-FAIL FUDGE

⅔ cup evaporated milk
1⅓ cups sugar
¼ teaspoon salt
¼ cup butter
16 large marshmallows, cut up
1½ cups semisweet chocolate chips
1 teaspoon vanilla
1 cup broken walnuts

Mix together milk, sugar, salt, butter, and marshmallows and bring to a boil, stirring constantly. Boil 5 minutes. Remove from heat. Add chocolate and stir until melted. Stir in vanilla and walnuts. Spread in buttered 8-inch square pan. Cool until firm.

Microwave TOFFEE

$^{1}/_{2}$ cup chopped pecans
$^{1}/_{2}$ cup (1 stick) butter
1 cup sugar
1 teaspoon salt
$^{1}/_{4}$ cup water
$^{1}/_{2}$ cup semisweet chocolate chips
$^{1}/_{4}$ cup chopped pecans

Sprinkle $^{1}/_{2}$ cup pecans in a 9-inch circle on a greased cookie sheet and set aside. Coat the top 2 inches of a 2-quart measuring cup with butter. Add butter, sugar, salt, and water; do not stir. Microwave on high (100%) for 10–11 minutes or until the mixture begins to turn light brown. Pour the mixture over the circle of pecans. Sprinkle with chocolate chips and let set for 1 minute. Spread the melted chips over toffee with knife and sprinkle with $^{1}/_{4}$ cup pecans. Chill until firm. Break into bite-sized pieces. Store in an airtight container.

Chocolate TRUFFLES

6 ounces semisweet baking chocolate,
   chopped
2 tablespoons butter
$\frac{1}{4}$ cup heavy whipping cream
1 tablespoon shortening
1 cup milk chocolate chips
Finely chopped nuts, shaved coconut,
   decorating candies (optional)

Line a cookie sheet with aluminum foil; set aside. In a medium saucepan, over low heat, melt baking chocolate, stirring constantly. Remove from heat. Stir in butter until completely melted. Add the whipping cream; stir. Refrigerate for 15–20 minutes, stirring frequently, until mixture is thick enough to hold shape. Drop the mixture by teaspoonfuls onto the prepared cookie sheet. Shape each one into a 1-inch ball. Freeze balls for 30 minutes. Heat the shortening and chocolate chips in a saucepan over low heat, stirring constantly, until the mixture is smooth; remove from heat. Dip each ball into the melted chocolate mixture. Place on foil-covered cookie sheet. Sprinkle chopped nuts, coconut, or decorating candies if desired. Refrigerate truffles for 10–15 minutes or until the coating is set. Serve at room temperature. Store in an airtight container in a cool, dry place.

Other things are just food.

But chocolate's chocolate!

PATRICK SKENE CATLING

German CHOCOLATE FUDGE

2 cups semisweet chocolate chips
12 (1-ounce) squares German sweet chocolate
1 (7-ounce) jar marshmallow crème
4½ cups sugar
2 tablespoons butter
1 (12-ounce) can evaporated milk
⅛ teaspoon salt
2 cups chopped pecans

Grease a 15x10x1-inch pan; set aside. Combine chocolate chips, German sweet chocolate, and marshmallow crème in large bowl; set aside. Combine sugar, butter, evaporated milk, and salt in a heavy skillet. Bring to a boil over medium heat. Cook for 6 minutes, stirring constantly. Pour hot syrup over the chocolate mixture. Stir until smooth. Stir in pecans. Pour mixture into the prepared pan. Let stand until firm; cut into squares.

Cherry SURPRISES

½ cup butter, softened
1 ¾ cups powdered sugar
1 teaspoon orange juice
1 ½ cups shredded coconut
1 (10-ounce) jar stemless maraschino
    cherries, drained

In a medium bowl, combine butter, powdered sugar, and orange juice. Stir in the coconut and mix until well combined. Wrap coconut mixture around each cherry to cover completely. Store in an airtight container in the refrigerator until ready to serve.

Festive FUDGE CUTOUTS

3 cups (1 ½ 12-ounce packages) semisweet
 chocolate chips
1 (14-ounce) can sweetened condensed milk
⅛ teaspoon salt
1 ½ teaspoons vanilla extract

Line a 9x13-inch pan with aluminum foil, extending the foil
over the edges of the pan. Place chocolate chips, sweetened
condensed milk, and salt in a large microwave-safe bowl.
Microwave on high (100%) for 1 minute; stir. Microwave on
high for an additional 20–30 seconds until chips are melted
and smooth when stirred. Stir in the vanilla. Pour mixture into
the prepared pan. Cover and refrigerate until firm. Use the foil
to lift the fudge out of the pan. Peel off foil and place onto a
cutting board. Using holiday cookie cutters, cut fudge into festive shapes. Store in an airtight container.

Variations
Use the following instead of chocolate chips for a variety of
fudge flavors:
PEANUT BUTTER FUDGE: Substitute 2 ½ cups peanut
butter chips.
WHITE CHOCOLATE FUDGE: Substitute 3 ½ cups white
chocolate chips.

Chocolate Caramel CANDY

1 cup milk chocolate chips
¼ cup butterscotch chips
¼ cup creamy peanut butter
¼ cup butter
1 cup sugar
¼ cup evaporated milk
1½ cups marshmallow crème
¼ cup creamy peanut butter
1 teaspoon vanilla extract
1½ cups chopped salted
   peanuts
14 ounces individually
   wrapped caramels,
   unwrapped
¼ cup heavy cream
¼ cup butterscotch chips
¼ cup creamy peanut butter
1 cup milk chocolate chips

Grease a 9x13-inch pan. Combine the chocolate chips, butterscotch chips, and peanut butter in a small saucepan. Cook over low heat, stirring constantly, until melted and smooth. Spread onto the bottom of the prepared pan. Refrigerate until set. In a heavy saucepan, melt the butter over medium heat. Stir in the sugar and evaporated milk. Bring the mixture to a boil and cook for 5 minutes, stirring constantly. Remove from heat and stir in the marshmallow crème, ¼ cup of peanut butter, and the vanilla. Add the peanuts and spread mixture over the cooled layer. Refrigerate until set. Combine the caramels and cream in a saucepan. Cook over low heat until melted, stirring constantly. Spread over the refrigerated layers. Refrigerate until set. In another saucepan, combine the last three ingredients. Cook over low heat, stirring constantly, until melted and smooth. Pour the mixture over the refrigerated caramel layer. Refrigerate for at least 1 hour. Cut into 1-inch squares. Store in the refrigerator.

Cookie BARK

1 (20-ounce) package chocolate sandwich cookies with
 cream filling
2 (18½-ounce) packages white chocolate

Line a 15x10x1-inch jelly roll pan with waxed paper. Coat paper with a non-stick cooking spray; set aside. Break half of the cookies into coarse pieces and place in a large bowl. In a microwave-safe bowl, melt one package of the white chocolate in the microwave. Quickly fold melted chocolate into the broken cookie pieces. Pour the mixture into the prepared pan and spread to cover half of the pan. Repeat the process with the remaining chocolate and cookies. Refrigerate until solid. Remove from the pan and carefully peel off the waxed paper. Place bark on a large cutting board and cut into pieces with a large knife. Store in an airtight container.

*My soul will be satisfied
as with the richest of foods;
with singing lips
my mouth will praise you.*

PSALM 63:5

Mocha FUDGE

2 cups (12-ounce package) semisweet
   chocolate chips
1 cup milk chocolate chips
2 tablespoons milk
1 (14-ounce) can sweetened condensed
   milk
4 teaspoons powdered instant coffee dissolved
   in 1 tablespoon warm water
1 tablespoon vanilla extract
1 cup chopped nuts

Line an 8-inch square pan with aluminum foil. Combine both
kinds of chips, milk, sweetened condensed milk, coffee, and
vanilla in a medium saucepan. Cook over low heat until chips
are melted, stirring constantly. Remove from the heat and stir
in nuts. Pour into the prepared pan and spread evenly with a
spatula. Refrigerate until firm. Remove from the pan and peel
off foil. Place onto a cutting board and cut into squares. Store
in an airtight container in the refrigerator.

Buckeyes

1 cup powdered sugar
$\frac{1}{2}$ cup creamy peanut butter
3 tablespoons butter or margarine
1 pound milk chocolate

In a large mixing bowl, stir together powdered sugar, peanut butter, and butter until well combined. Shape into about 30 1-inch balls. Place balls on a baking sheet lined with waxed paper. Let stand for about 25 minutes or until dry. Place water in the bottom of a double boiler to within $\frac{1}{2}$-inch of upper pan. Make sure the upper pan does not touch the water. While balls are cooling and water is heating, finely chop the chocolate so it will melt quickly. Bring the water to a boil. Remove from heat and place about $\frac{1}{4}$ of the chocolate in the top of the double boiler. Stir until melted. Add about $\frac{1}{2}$ cup more, stir, and repeat until all chocolate is melted. Stir until chocolate reaches 120°; reheat if necessary to reach this temperature. After chocolate has reached 120°, refill bottom of the double boiler with cool water to within $\frac{1}{2}$ inch of upper pan. Stir frequently until chocolate cools to 83°. This should take about 30 minutes. Using a toothpick, dip balls in chocolate, working quickly and stirring chocolate frequently to keep it evenly heated. Place balls on cookie sheet. (Chocolate will stay close to 83° for about 30 minutes. If temperature falls below 80°, chocolate must be remelted.) Store tightly covered in a cool, dry place.

Cream Cheese MINTS

1 (3-ounce) package cream cheese, softened
1 tablespoon butter, softened
3 cups powdered sugar
2 drops peppermint oil
Any color food coloring (optional)

In a large bowl, combine cream cheese, butter, and powdered sugar. Stir in peppermint oil. Color as desired with food coloring or leave white. Roll the cream cheese mixture into small balls and place on a sheet of waxed paper. Flatten with a fork dipped in powdered sugar. Let dry for about 2 hours on waxed paper, then freeze or refrigerate.

Pineapple FUDGE

1 cup evaporated milk
3 cups sugar
2 tablespoons butter
1 cup crushed pineapple, drained
2 teaspoons lemon juice

Grease a 9-inch square pan; set aside. In a saucepan, combine evaporated milk, sugar, and butter. Heat to boiling. Stir in pineapple and heat to soft-ball stage (236°), stirring constantly for about 25 minutes. Remove from heat and allow to cool. Stir in lemon juice and beat until mixture is smooth. Pour into the prepared pan. Allow to cool completely before cutting into squares.

Nothing is sweeter than

Christ in your life.

Chocolate-Covered ORANGE BALLS

1 pound powdered sugar
1 (12-ounce) package vanilla wafers, crushed
1 cup chopped walnuts
¼ pound butter
1 (6-ounce) can frozen orange juice
    concentrate, thawed
1½ pounds milk chocolate chips, melted

In a large bowl, combine the powdered sugar, vanilla wafers, walnuts, butter, and orange juice. Mix well and shape into 1-inch balls. Place balls on a sheet of waxed paper and allow to dry for 1 hour. Place chocolate chips in the top of a double boiler. Stir frequently over medium heat until melted. Dip balls into the melted chocolate and place in decorative paper cups. Allow to cool completely before serving.

Cheery Cherry CHRISTMAS FUDGE

1 (8-ounce) can almond paste
1 (14-ounce) can sweetened condensed milk,
    divided
Red food coloring
1 3/4 cups semisweet chocolate chips
Red candied cherry halves
Sliced almonds

Line an 8-inch square pan with aluminum foil, extending the foil over the edges of the pan. Beat almond paste and 1/4 cup sweetened condensed milk in a small bowl until it is well mixed. Add food coloring and beat until blended. Refrigerate for about 1 hour or until firm. Spread onto the bottom of prepared pan. Place chocolate chips and the remaining sweetened condensed milk in a medium microwave-safe bowl. Microwave on high (100%) for 1–1 1/2 minutes or until chocolate is melted and smooth. Spread over top of the almond paste layer. Cover, and refrigerate until firm. Use the edges of the foil to lift out of the pan. Peel off the foil and cut fudge into squares. Garnish with cherry halves and sliced almonds. Store in an airtight container in the refrigerator.

Cherry NUT BALLS

1 cup butter, softened
1 cup powdered sugar
1 teaspoon vanilla
$^{1}/_{2}$ cup maraschino cherries,
   chopped

$^{3}/_{4}$ cup coconut
2 cups uncooked oats
Fincly ground nuts to roll
   balls in

Beat the butter, sugar, vanilla, cherries, and coconut in a large bowl. Mix in the oats. Cover, and refrigerate for 3 hours. Shape the mixture into 1-inch balls. Roll each ball in the chopped nuts. Store in an airtight container.

Ice Cream FUDGE

2 pounds semisweet chocolate, chopped
1 pint mint ice cream, slightly thawed
1 cup chopped pecans

Line a 9-inch square pan with aluminum foil. Lightly grease the foil. Place the chocolate in a large microwave-safe bowl. Microwave on high (100%) for 1 minute and 45 seconds; stir. Add the thawed ice cream and beat until smooth. Stir in the pecans. Pour into the prepared pan. Refrigerate until fudge is firm. Cut into squares and store in an airtight container in the refrigerator.

Cookies

Nard and saffron,
calamus and cinnamon,
with every kind of incense tree,
with myrrh and aloes
and all the finest spices. . .

SONG OF SONGS 4:14

Nothing warms a home like a fire on the hearth and fresh cookies in the oven. Light those logs, then tie on your apron.

Decorate some to create a pretty platter for a buffet table, make some for gifts, or let the kids get involved. Whatever appeals to you, don't miss out on a traditional and fun way to celebrate the Christmas holiday!

NO-BAKE  COOKIES

$^1\!/_2$ cup (1 stick) butter or margarine,
   cut into pieces
$^1\!/_2$ cup milk
2 cups sugar
$^1\!/_3$ cup cocoa powder
1 teaspoon salt
1 teaspoon vanilla extract
4 cups quick-cooking oats

Line a tray or cookie sheet with waxed paper. Combine butter and milk in a large microwave-safe bowl. Microwave on high (100%) for 1 minute or until butter is melted. Stir in the sugar and cocoa until mixed. Microwave on high for $1^1\!/_2$ minutes; stir. Microwave on high an additional $1^1\!/_2$–3 minutes or until sugar is completely dissolved. Stir in salt, vanilla, and oats. Drop by spoonfuls onto prepared tray or cookie sheet. Flatten slightly and let stand until firm. Makes 3 dozen.

Sweet as ANGELS' KISSES

4 egg whites, room temperature
$1/4$ teaspoon cream of tartar
$1/8$ teaspoon salt
1 cup sugar
$1/4$ teaspoon peppermint extract
A few drops of red food coloring

Beat egg whites until foamy. Add cream of tartar and salt; beat until soft peaks form. Add sugar, beating until stiff peaks form. Mix in peppermint extract and food coloring. Drop rounded tablespoons of mixture onto parchment paper or foil-lined cookie sheets. Bake at 250° for 35–45 minutes or until cookies are firm to the touch and just beginning to brown around the edges. Remove from oven and cool.

 Red RIBBONS

Red ribbons add color and beauty to a cookie assortment.

1 cup butter, softened
2 ½ cups all-purpose flour
½ cup sugar
1 egg, slightly beaten
1 teaspoon vanilla

¼ teaspoon salt
Strawberry jam or raspberry jelly
Water
¾ cup confectioners' sugar

Beat the butter with an electric mixer on medium to high speed for 30 seconds. Add about half of the flour, then the sugar, egg, vanilla, and salt. Beat until thoroughly mixed. Add in the remaining flour, mixing until the dough sticks together to form a ball. Lightly knead ball. Divide the cookie dough into 8 equal portions. On a lightly floured surface, roll each portion of dough into a 9-inch rope. Place the ropes on an ungreased cookie sheet about 2 inches apart. Press a groove down the length of each rope with the handle of a wooden spoon. Bake in a 375° oven for 10 minutes. Spoon jam or jelly into groove and bake until edges begin to brown slightly (about 5 minutes). Cool on cookie sheet for 5 minutes. Using a large spatula, remove cookies to a cutting board. Mix water and confectioners' sugar to form a glaze. Drizzle over hot cookies. Cut into 1-inch slices. Move cookies to wire rack to finish cooling.

Chocolate-Striped COOKIES

½ cup butter
½ cup shortening
1 cup sugar
½ teaspoon baking soda
⅛ teaspoon salt
1 egg
2 tablespoons milk
1 teaspoon vanilla

3 cups all-purpose flour
⅓ cup semisweet chocolate pieces,
   melted and cooled
½ cup finely chopped nuts
½ cup miniature semisweet
   chocolate pieces
¼ teaspoon almond extract

Beat butter and shortening on medium to high speed for 30 seconds. Add sugar, baking soda, and salt; beat until combined. Beat in the egg, milk, and vanilla. Beat in as much of the flour as you can with the mixer, then stir in remaining flour by hand. Divide dough in half. Knead the melted chocolate and nuts into half of the dough. Knead the miniature chocolate pieces and almond extract into the other half of dough. Divide each portion of dough in half. Line the bottom and sides of a 9x5x3-inch loaf pan with plastic wrap. Press half of the chocolate dough evenly in pan. Layer in the vanilla, the remaining chocolate, then the last vanilla to form four even, flat layers. Invert pan to remove dough and peel off plastic wrap. Cut dough crosswise into ¼-inch-thick slices. Place cookies 2 inches apart on an ungreased cookie sheet. Bake cookies at 375° for about 10 minutes.

Tip: *This dough can be made and frozen in a plastic freezer bag up to a month in advance.*

Lemon Nut STAR COOKIES

These are colorful, fun, and delicious, too!
At Christmastime, use red and green food coloring
and white (untinted) glaze for festive-looking cookies.

Cookies:

1 cup butter, softened

2 cups powdered sugar

2 eggs

2 tablespoons lemon juice

4 teaspoons half-and-half cream

2 teaspoons grated lemon peel

3 1/4 cups flour

1/2 cup finely ground almonds

1/2 teaspoon baking soda

1/8 teaspoon salt

Cream butter and powdered sugar. Add eggs, one at a time. Beat well. Blend in lemon juice, cream, and lemon peel. Combine and gradually add flour, almonds, baking soda, and salt. Cover and refrigerate for 2–3 hours or until firm. On a lightly floured surface, roll dough to $\frac{1}{8}$-inch thickness. Cut into stars with a cookie cutter. Bake at 350° for 8–10 minutes or until lightly browned.

Glaze:

2 cups powdered sugar	2 tablespoons lemon juice
$\frac{1}{4}$ cup light corn syrup	Red and green food coloring

Stir powdered sugar, corn syrup, and lemon juice until smooth. Divide into 3 bowls. Tint one portion red, one green, and leave one plain. Spread over cookies. Allow to harden overnight.

Tip: *These make great Fourth of July cookies when iced with red, white, or blue glaze.*

*After Jesus was born
in Bethlehem in Judea,
during the time of King Herod,
Magi from the east came
to Jerusalem and asked,
"Where is the one who has been
born king of the Jews?
We saw his star in the east
and have come to worship him."*

MATTHEW 2:1–2

Candy Cane TWISTIES

½ cup butter, softened
½ cup shortening
1 cup sugar
¼ cup powdered sugar
½ cup milk
1 egg

1 teaspoon peppermint
  extract
1 teaspoon vanilla extract
3 ½ cups flour
¼ teaspoon salt
Green and red food
  coloring

Cream butter, shortening, and sugars. Blend in milk, egg, and extracts. Gradually add flour and salt. Set aside half of dough. Divide remaining dough in half, adding green food coloring to one portion and red to the other. Wrap dough separately in plastic wrap. Refrigerate for 1 hour or until easy to handle. Roll ½ teaspoonfuls of each color of dough into 3-inch ropes. Place each green rope next to a white rope; press together gently and twist. Repeat with red ropes and remaining white ropes. Place 2 inches apart on ungreased baking sheets. Curve one end, forming a cane. Bake at 350° for 11–13 minutes or until set. Cool for 2 minutes; carefully remove to wire racks.

Christmas WREATHS

1/2 cup butter
30 large marshmallows
1 1/2 teaspoons green food coloring
1 teaspoon vanilla extract
4 cups cornflakes cereal
2 tablespoons cinnamon candies

Melt the butter in a large saucepan over low heat. Add the marshmallows, and heat until completely melted, stirring constantly. Remove from heat, and add the food coloring, vanilla, and cornflakes. With lightly greased fingers, quickly drop spoonfuls of the mixture onto waxed paper, and form it into the shape of a wreath. Immediately decorate with the cinnamon candies. Allow to cool at room temperature before removing from waxed paper. Store in an airtight container.

Buckeyes

(From the kitchen of Carolyn Boone)
These disappear fast!

Filling:

2 pounds peanut butter   1 pound butter
3 pounds powdered sugar

Mix well. Chill until firm. Roll into 1-inch balls.

Icing:

2 packages chocolate chips (12 ounces)
$\frac{1}{2}$ bar paraffin wax

Melt in double boiler. Using toothpick, dip balls in chocolate, leaving just the top uncovered. Cool on waxed paper.

Tip: *Buckeyes are best made with a heavy-duty mixer.*

Chunky CHOCOLATE COOKIES

Sweeter and chunkier than the traditional chocolate chip cookie.

1 4-ounce bar of sweet chocolate
$\frac{1}{2}$ cup butter
$\frac{1}{2}$ cup sugar
$\frac{1}{4}$ cup brown sugar
1 egg

1 teaspoon vanilla
1 cup all-purpose flour
$\frac{1}{2}$ teaspoon baking soda
$\frac{1}{2}$ teaspoon salt
$\frac{1}{2}$ cup coarsely chopped
  nuts

Chop chocolate bar into bite-sized pieces; set aside. Cream butter until soft. Add sugars, egg, and vanilla; beat until light and fluffy. Add flour, soda, and salt. Stir in chocolate pieces and nuts. Drop by teaspoonfuls 2 inches apart onto cookie sheet. Bake at 375° for 8–10 minutes or until lightly browned.

 SUGAR COOKIES

(From the kitchen of Betty Young)

2 eggs	³/₄ cup sugar
²/₃ cup oil	2 teaspoons baking powder
2 teaspoons vanilla	2 cups flour
1 teaspoon grated lemon rind	¹/₂ teaspoon salt

Beat eggs and stir in oil, vanilla, and lemon. Blend in sugar and beat until thick. Add dry ingredients. Drop 2 inches apart on ungreased cookie sheet. Flatten with glass dipped in oil and sugar. Bake at 400° for 8–10 minutes.

CHUNKY *Peanut Butter*

CHOCOLATE CHUNK COOKIES

(From the kitchen of Diane Pershing)

8 tablespoons (unsalted) butter at room
temperature
$\frac{1}{4}$ cup granulated sugar
$\frac{3}{4}$ cup packed dark brown sugar
1 teaspoon vanilla extract
$\frac{1}{4}$ teaspoon salt
$\frac{1}{3}$ cup chunky-style peanut butter
1 egg
$\frac{1}{2}$ teaspoon baking soda
1 cup all-purpose flour
$\frac{3}{4}$ cup (about 4 ounces) coarsely
chopped unsalted roasted peanuts
12 ounces (2 cups) coarsely chopped semisweet
chocolate bars (4 3-ounce bars, such as Lindt
or Tobler)
Vegetable shortening for baking sheets

Combine the butter, sugar, brown sugar, vanilla, and salt. Beat with a spoon until fluffy. Beat in the peanut butter, egg, and baking soda. Stir in the flour and then the peanuts and chocolate. Transfer to a bowl just large enough to hold the dough. Cover and refrigerate until firm, about 4 hours or overnight. Lightly coat 1 or 2 baking sheets with vegetable shortening. Using 1 tablespoon of dough for each cookie, shape the dough into balls. Place 12 cookies per sheet. Bake at 350° for 10 minutes, until the cookies spring back when very lightly touched. Do not overbake or the cookies will dry out. Cool on the sheets for 2 minutes, then transfer to paper towel for about 2 minutes, and finally transfer to a rack to cool.

Lemon Snowflake COOKIES

1 package lemon cake mix with pudding
1 egg
2 1/4 cups frozen whipped topping, thawed
2 cups powdered sugar

Mix the cake mix, egg, and whipped topping together. Beat with an electric mixer on medium speed until well blended and sticky. Drop one teaspoonful batter into the powdered sugar and roll to coat. Place cookies onto ungreased sheets. Bake at 350° for 8–10 minutes or until lightly browned.

MARSHMALLOW No-Bake COOKIES

1 cup sugar
1 cup light corn syrup
4 cups cornflakes cereal
12 ounces creamy peanut butter
1 cup semisweet chocolate chips
1 cup miniature marshmallows

In a large saucepan, combine the sugar and light corn syrup; cook over low heat until the sugar is dissolved. Remove from heat. Stir in the cornflakes and peanut butter. Fold in chocolate chips and marshmallows. Stir until thoroughly mixed. Drop by rounded teaspoonfuls onto waxed paper and allow to cool until firm. Store in an airtight container.

Christmas Tree SPICE COOKIES

1 cup butter	2 teaspoons ground ginger
1 cup sugar	4 $\frac{1}{2}$ cups flour
1 large egg	$\frac{1}{2}$ teaspoon salt
$\frac{1}{2}$ cup honey	1 teaspoon cinnamon
$\frac{3}{4}$ teaspoon baking powder	Colored sugar sprinkles (optional)

Cream butter and sugar. Add egg and honey; continue beating until light and fluffy. Mix in dry ingredients (except colored sugar). Cover and chill dough for one hour. Roll out dough to $\frac{1}{4}$-inch thickness. Cut with 3–3 $\frac{1}{2}$-inch tree-shaped cookie cutter. Place on lightly greased cookie sheet. Sprinkle with colored sugar. Bake at 375° for 10–12 minutes or until cookies are golden.

Tip: *Tree-shaped cookie cutters make this quick and simple!*

DECORATING *Ideas*

* Add a few drops of food coloring into the dough to brighten your cookies. Green makes pretty trees, holly leaves, and wreaths. A drop of yellow can make the lemon cookie look more vibrant.

* Add food coloring to white icing as desired in small amounts at a time. You can also buy tubes of already-colored icings. The gel tubes are easy to use and look wonderful, but a word of caution: They don't dry and are liable to smear!

* A cake-decorating paper or plastic cone with inter-changeable tips adds a polished look to festive cookies.

DECORATING *Designs*

* Ice a tree in white or pale green, then pipe or drizzle horizontal, dark green stripes. Take a knife or toothpick and stripe upward in the center from trunk to tip, forming boughs.

* Spread white frosting over a simple circle, then add red striping around the edges—viola! A peppermint candy!

* A giant square cookie can be iced, then decorated to become a giant Christmas card.

* A quick, simple dusting of powdered sugar adds sweetness and a snowy look.

 Jolly SNOWMAN COOKIES

This is so simple to do, and even the littlest helpers can be part of the fun. Shoestring licorice turns into a snowman's top hat on these iced sugar cookies.

Directions:
Using a favorite rolled cookie recipe, simply cut into circles with a cookie cutter, or roll dough and slice.

Once cookies are cooled:

1 tub of ready-to spread frosting	⅓ cup raisins
Black shoestring licorice	¼ cup red cinnamon candies

Ice cookies:
Put frosting on each cookie. Cut licorice into pieces—some longer than others. Place licorice over top third of cookie to create hat. (Use longer pieces to create brim that overhangs cookie edges and shorter pieces to fit within cookie.) Use raisins for eyes and nose (1–3 pieces depending on cookie size) and 5 red candies for mouth.

Tip: *This is easiest if one cookie is frosted at a time and then decorated— especially for little fingers.*

Shortbread

(From the kitchen of Vanessa Kealy,
who received this recipe from a friend in Scotland.
This is exactly the way she measured and prepared them.)

16 tablespoons flour—scoop & shake
4 tablespoons sugar
8 tablespoons butter—1 cube set out a bit (margarine
will not work)

Mix flour and sugar, then gradually squish in butter. Knead until dough forms a big ball. Flour board and roll out an 8x6-inch rectangle about ¼-inch thick. Using a knife, cut into 2x1-inch strips. Place 1 inch apart on an ungreased baking sheet. Dip fork in flour and prick holes. Bake at 325°, nice and slow. Check in 30–40 minutes. Bottom of shortbread will be pale brown. Remove from oven and let sit. Sprinkle with sugar.

 BAKKELSER

A Norwegian holiday favorite!

10 egg yolks
$^1/_3$ cup powdered sugar
$^1/_2$ cup whipping cream
1 tablespoon brandy
1 teaspoon ground cardamom
$^1/_2$ teaspoon grated lemon peel
2–2 $^1/_2$ cups flour
Oil for frying

Beat egg yolks and sugar until very thick and lemon-colored (about 10 minutes). Add in cream, brandy, cardamom, and lemon peel. Mix in enough flour until dough is stiff. Chill 3–4 hours. Heat oil to 375°. Divide dough in half. Roll very thin, $^1/_8$–$^1/_{16}$-inch thick. Cut dough into 4x2-inch diamonds. Make a 1-inch slit in center of each. Draw long point of diamond through slit and curl back in opposite direction. Fry in hot fat about 15 seconds on each side, or until light brown. Drain, then sprinkle with powdered sugar. Store in airtight container.

Cocoa Nut DROP COOKIES

1 cup sugar
1/4 cup butter
1 egg
1/2 cup milk
1 1/2 cups flour
2 teaspoons baking powder
1/2 cup cocoa
1 cup chopped nuts

Cream sugar and butter together. Beat egg, then add the egg and milk to sugar and butter mixture. Sift flour, baking powder, and cocoa. Add to mixture. Add nuts and stir well. Drop with spoon onto greased cookie sheet. Bake at 375° for 15 minutes.

Persimmon COOKIES

½ cup shortening
1 cup sugar
1 egg
1 cup pureed persimmon pulp
2 cups flour
1 teaspoon baking soda
½ teaspoon nutmeg

1 teaspoon cinnamon
1 teaspoon baking powder
¼ teaspoon salt
¼ teaspoon clove
1 cup golden raisins
1 cup chopped nuts

Cream shortening, sugar, and egg. Add persimmon pulp and mix well. Add dry ingredients. Mix in raisins and nuts. Drop by teaspoonful onto ungreased cookie sheet. These cookies don't spread. Bake at 350° for 12 minutes or until they just spring back when touched.

Orange Cranberry DROPS

½ cup white sugar
½ cup packed brown sugar
¼ cup butter, softened
1 egg
3 tablespoons orange juice
½ teaspoon orange extract
1 teaspoon orange zest
1½ cups flour
½ teaspoon baking powder
¼ teaspoon baking soda
¼ teaspoon salt
1 cup dried cranberries

Cream together the white sugar, brown sugar, and butter. Stir in the egg, orange juice, orange extract, and orange zest. Sift together the flour, baking powder, baking soda, and salt. Stir dry ingredients into the orange mixture. Fold in the dried cranberries. Drop heaping teaspoonfuls 2 inches apart on greased cookie sheet. Bake at 375° for 10–12 minutes or until edges begin to brown. Cool on baking sheets or remove to cool on wire racks.

Grandmother's OATMEAL RAISIN

(From the kitchen of Helen Fonti)

¾ cup flour
½ teaspoon baking soda
¼ teaspoon salt
½ cup butter
½ cup granulated sugar

⅓ cup packed brown sugar
1 large egg
2 teaspoons vanilla extract
½ cup uncooked oatmeal
¾ cup dark seedless raisins

Combine flour, baking soda, and salt. In separate large bowl, beat butter and sugars until light and fluffy. Beat in egg and vanilla until well blended. Add in flour mixture; stir until well blended, but do not overbeat. Stir in oatmeal and raisins with wooden spoon. Drop heaping tablespoons of dough on ungreased cookie sheets. Bake at 350° for 15 minutes.

Lemon YUMMIES

(From the kitchen of Sharon Kay Smith,
who received Cook, Hospitality, and
Foods Girl Scout Badges with this recipe in 1955.)

1 cup shortening	1 tablespoon grated
½ cup brown sugar	lemon rind
½ cup granulated sugar	2 cups flour
1 egg, well beaten	½ teaspoon salt
2 tablespoons lemon juice	¼ teaspoon baking soda
	½ cup chopped nut meats

Cream the shortening, and add the sugars gradually. Add the egg, lemon juice, and rind, and mix well. Add the sifted dry ingredients and nut meats, and mix thoroughly. Form into a roll about 2 inches in diameter, wrap in waxed paper, and chill in the refrigerator. Cut into ¼-inch slices and bake on cookie sheets. Bake at 375° for 8–10 minutes.

A balanced diet is

a cookie in each hand.

AUTHOR UNKNOWN

 Butterhorn COOKIES

(From the kitchen of Luisa Stoner)

2 cubes butter	1 egg yolk
2 ½ cups flour	¾ cup sour cream

Cinnamon Mix:

¾ cup sugar	¾ cup chopped
1 teaspoon cinnamon	almonds

Work butter into flour with fingers. Add egg yolk and sour cream, blending well. Shape into ball, sprinkle with flour, and wrap with waxed paper. Chill for several hours or days (the longer the better). Divide chilled dough into 4 pieces and roll one at a time with rolling pin into a circle as if making a piecrust. Roll out to ⅛-inch thickness. Sprinkle with cinnamon mixture and cut into pieces as if cutting a pie. (Be sure to use lots of cinnamon mix.) Roll each piece as if making a crescent roll. Set on greased cookie sheet. Bake at 350° for 20–30 minutes, or until golden brown. Remove quickly from pan and let cool on breadboard or any cold surface.

Helpful Tip: *Prepare all your cookies first, before you start baking.*

 All-Night KISSES

2 egg whites
Dash of salt
¾ cup sugar
1 6-ounce package of butterscotch,
    chocolate, or mint chocolate chips

Preheat oven to 350°. Beat egg whites and salt until stiff. Gradually add sugar. Fold in flavored chips. Drop by teaspoonfuls onto ungreased cookie sheet—these stay in shape they are dropped, so form into candy kiss shape. Put in oven and close door. **Turn oven off!** Do not open oven door until morning!

CHRISTMAS *Blessing* COOKIES

These cookies can be packed in Chinese takeout containers and given as a gift.

$1/2$ cup cake flour	4 tablespoons cooking oil
2 tablespoons cornstarch	2 egg whites
4 tablespoons sugar	2 tablespoons water
Dash salt	2 drops red food coloring

Sift together the dry ingredients and add salt. Add oil and egg whites; stir until smooth. Add water and food coloring; mix well. Make one cookie at a time by pouring 1 tablespoon batter onto lightly greased skillet. Spread to $3^{1}/_{2}$-inch circle. Cook over low heat for 4 minutes or until lightly browned. Flip with spatula and cook 1 more minute. Slide out onto pot holder and work swiftly: Put blessing in center, fold cookie in half, then bend in half over edge of a bowl. Place in a muffin pan to cool.

Tip: *Write blessings and Bible verses on strips of paper before mixing the recipe.*

Butterscotch DROPS

1 ⅔ cups butterscotch chips   5 ½ cups cornflakes cereal
1 cup creamy peanut butter

Line two baking sheets with waxed paper. Place the butterscotch chips in a microwave-safe bowl. Microwave on medium-high (70%) for 1 minute; stir. Microwave at additional 10-second intervals until melted and smooth. Stir in the peanut butter until smooth. Add the cornflakes and mix until evenly coated. Drop mixture by rounded spoonfuls onto the prepared baking sheets. Refrigerate for 20 minutes or until firm. Store in an airtight container in the refrigerator.

Swedish TEA COOKIES

(From the kitchen of Tracie Peterson)
*Give these in a basket and fill with special tins of tea and honey.
And maybe a teacup, too!*

1 cup butter	3 $^1\!/_2$ cups flour, sifted
2 cups brown sugar	1 teaspoon baking soda
2 eggs	$^1\!/_2$ teaspoon salt
	1 cup chopped nuts

Cream the butter and sugar. Add the eggs. Sift the flour with the baking soda and salt. Add the nuts. Roll into a tube. Chill for at least 2 hours. Slice thinly. Bake at 350° for 7–10 minutes.

Butterscotch GINGERBREAD MEN

½ cup butter, softened
½ cup packed brown sugar
1 small package instant butterscotch pudding mix
1 egg
1½ cups flour
1½ teaspoons ground ginger
½ teaspoon baking soda
½ teaspoon ground cinnamon

Icing:

2 cups powdered sugar   Assorted decorator candies
3 tablespoons milk   Raisins

Cream butter, brown sugar, and pudding mix. Add egg. Combine flour, ginger, baking soda, and cinnamon; gradually add to the creamed mixture. Cover and refrigerate overnight. On a lightly floured surface, roll out to ⅛-inch thickness. Cut with a 5-inch gingerbread man cutter. Place 1 inch apart on ungreased baking sheets. Bake at 350° for 8–10 minutes or until edges are golden. Remove to wire racks to cool. Combine powdered sugar and milk until smooth. Frost and decorate cookies with candies and raisins.

Mexican CHRISTMAS COOKIES

2 tablespoons cinnamon
2 cups sugar
2 cups butter or shortening
1 tablespoon whole anise seed
1 cup fruit juice
2 egg yolks
4 cups sifted flour

In a large bowl, combine 1 tablespoon cinnamon and 1 cup of the sugar with the remaining ingredients. Stir until well blended. Chill covered for at least 1 hour; overnight is best. Roll dough out 1/4-inch thick on a well-floured surface. Cut into 1-inch circles. Place on greased cookie sheet. Bake at 350° for 15 minutes, or until light brown. In a large bowl, combine the remaining sugar and cinnamon. Drop the warm cookies into the sugar mixture then place on a rack to cool.

Snowballs

2 1/4 cups chocolate sandwich cookie crumbs
1 cup pecans, finely chopped
1 1/2 cups powdered sugar, sifted and divided
1/3 cup coconut flakes
1/4 cup light corn syrup
1/4 cup strawberry preserves

In a large bowl, combine cookie crumbs, pecans, 1/4 cup powdered sugar, and coconut; mix well. Stir in the corn syrup and preserves. Shape the mixture into 1-inch balls. Roll each ball in the remaining powdered sugar. Store in an airtight container.

Cathedral WINDOWS

¼ cup butter
2 cups semisweet chocolate chips
2 eggs, beaten
1 cup chopped pecans
1 (10½-ounce) package colored miniature
    marshmallows
⅓ cup powdered sugar for decoration

Line a 9x5-inch loaf pan with foil; set aside. Place butter and chocolate chips in a microwave-safe bowl. Microwave until melted, stirring frequently. Stir in the eggs, pecans, and colored marshmallows. Pour the mixture into the prepared pan. Dust with powdered sugar and refrigerate until firm. Remove chilled dough from loaf pan, gently peel off the foil, and slice into ¼-inch slices.

 Holiday ICED COOKIES

Cookies:

⅓ cup vegetable shortening
⅓ cup butter
¾ cup sugar
1 egg
1 tablespoon milk

1 teaspoon vanilla
1 teaspoon baking powder
2 cups flour
¼ teaspoon salt

Cream shortening, butter, sugar until fluffy. Add egg, milk, vanilla until combined. Combine dry ingredients and add slowly until well mixed. Divide dough in half. Cover and chill 3 hours or until dough is firm. On a lightly floured surface, roll ½ the dough to ⅛-inch thickness. Cut dough with cookie cutters into desired holiday shapes: stars, trees, bells, holly, etc. Bake at 375° for 7–8 minutes or until edges are firm and bottoms are lightly browned.

Icing:

1 cup powdered sugar
¼ teaspoon vanilla

1 tablespoon milk
Food coloring (optional)

In a small mixing bowl stir powdered sugar, vanilla, and enough of the milk to make icing a piping consistency. Different-colored icings can be made by adding a few drops of food coloring. Use a pastry bag and writing tips to decorate cookies.

*When decorating cookies, always have graham
crackers and pretzels around so you can use up the
leftover icing to make graham sandwiches or dip
the pretzels in the last bit of melted chocolate.*

Pecan DAINTIES

These delightful cookies are reminiscent of pecan pie.

Cheese Pastry:

    1 3-ounce package of cream cheese   1 cup sifted flour
    ½ cup butter

Blend cream cheese and butter. Stir in flour. Chill one hour. Shape into 2 dozen 1 inch balls. Place in ungreased muffin tin and thumbprint the dough to create indentation for filling.

Pecan Filling:

    1 egg   ¾ cup brown sugar
    1 tablespoon butter   1 teaspoon vanilla
    Dash of salt   ⅔ cup chopped pecans

Beat all ingredients (except pecans) until smooth. Divide ½ of pecans among pastry. Top with mixture. Top with remaining pecans. Bake at 350° for 25 minutes.

Tip: *The easiest way to keep these cookies uniform is to use a 1 ¾-inch muffin tin, but they can be made on a regular cookie sheet.*

Amaretti

These almond macaroons are an Italian favorite.

2 egg whites
1 teaspoon vanilla
$\frac{1}{2}$ teaspoon almond extract
1 $\frac{1}{2}$ cups blanched almonds, finely chopped
    (about 8 ounces)
1 cup powdered sugar, sifted

Beat egg whites, vanilla, and almond extract until stiff peaks form. Combine almonds and powdered sugar, then fold into egg white mixture. Drop by teaspoonfuls onto greased cookie sheet (or on cookie sheet lined with parchment paper). Bake at 325° for 15–20 minutes, until lightly browned. For crisper cookies, turn off oven, open door, and let dry for another 10–15 minutes.

 *Sugar* COOKIES

²/₃ cup butter
³/₄ cup sugar
1 egg
1 teaspoon vanilla

4 teaspoons milk
¼ teaspoon salt
1 ½ teaspoons baking
    powder
2 cups flour

Cream butter and sugar until fluffy. Blend in egg, vanilla, and milk. Combine dry ingredients and mix well. Divide dough in half and chill 1 hour. Roll dough ⅛-inch thick on lightly floured surface and cut with cookie cutters, or roll into tube and slice. Bake at 375° for 6–8 minutes, or until edges begin to brown.

Caramel SHORTBREAD

Base:

    1 cup butter
    ¹/₂ cup sifted icing sugar

    ¹/₄ teaspoon salt
    1¹/₄ cups flour

Beat butter, sugar, and salt until fluffy. Add flour. Spread in a greased 9-inch pan. Bake at 350° for 30 minutes.

Topping:

    ¹/₂ cup butter
    1 can sweetened condensed milk
    3 tablespoons honey
    1 teaspoon vanilla
    2 squares semisweet chocolate, melted

Melt butter in microwave. Stir in milk and honey. Cook on high for 6–8 minutes until caramel color, stirring after each minute. Add vanilla. Spread over shortbread, drizzle with melted chocolate, and chill until firm.

Oatmeal Chocolate CHIP COOKIES

1 cup butter
1 cup brown sugar
1 cup sugar
2 eggs
1 teaspoon vanilla
2 cups flour
2½ cups blended oatmeal (Measure and blend to
   a fine powder in blender or food processor.)
½ teaspoon salt
1 teaspoon baking soda
1 teaspoon baking powder
2 cups (12 ounces) chocolate chips
1 4-ounce Hershey Bar, grated
1½ cups chopped walnuts

Cream butter with both sugars until fluffy. Add eggs and vanilla; mix together with flour, oatmeal, salt, baking soda, and baking powder. Add chocolate chips, Hershey Bar, and nuts. Roll into balls and place 2 inches apart on cookie sheet. Bake at 375° for 10 minutes.

Super Easy

PEANUT BUTTER COOKIES

(From the kitchen of Betty Young)
No flour, salt, or anything. Enjoy!

1 cup peanut butter (crunchy or creamy)
1 cup sugar
1 egg

Mix all together well. Roll into about 1-inch balls, then criss-cross with fork. Bake at 350° for about 10 minutes or until golden brown.

Through Jesus, therefore,
let us continually offer to God
a sacrifice of praise—
the fruit of lips that confess his name.
And do not forget to do good
and to share with others,
for with such sacrifices God is pleased.

HEBREWS 13:15–16

Ginger Cream COOKIES

(From the kitchen of Cindy Malinowski)
This recipe dates back to the 1880s.
For Christmas, decorate them with colored sugars.

$\frac{1}{2}$ cup shortening
1 cup sugar
2 eggs
1 cup molasses
4 cups flour
1 teaspoon salt

2 teaspoons ground ginger
1 teaspoon ground cloves
1 teaspoon cinnamon
2 teaspoons baking soda
1 cup hot water

Cream the shortening, sugar, and eggs. Add the molasses. Sift dry ingredients together, except for the baking soda. Dissolve the soda in the hot water; then add alternately to the dry ingredients. Chill the dough thoroughly. Drop by teaspoon onto greased cookie sheets 2 inches apart. Bake at 400° for 8 minutes. While still warm, ice with a thin white frosting.

Snickerdoodle COOKIES

(From the kitchen of Vickie McDonough)

1 cup shortening (or $1/2$ cup
    shortening and $1/2$ cup butter)
$1 1/2$ cups white sugar
2 eggs

1 teaspoon baking soda
$1/4$ teaspoon salt
$2 3/4$ cups flour
2 teaspoons cream of tartar

Coating:
2 tablespoons sugar

2 teaspoons cinnamon

Berlinerkranzer

These little Norwegian wreath cookies are a traditional favorite.

Dough:

³/₄ cup butter, softened
¹/₄ cup shortening
1 cup sugar

2 teaspoons grated orange
    peel
2 eggs
4 cups flour

Cream butter, shortening, and sugar. Add orange peel and eggs. Mix in flour. Roll dough by rounded teaspoonfuls into ropes about 6 inches long. Form each rope into a circle, bringing one end over and through into a single knot (kind of like a shoelace). Let ends extend ¹/₂ inch. Place on ungreased cookie sheet.

Glaze and decoration:

1 egg white
2 tablespoons sugar

Red candied cherries
Green candied citron

Beat egg white until foamy, adding sugar 1 tablespoon at a time. Brush tops of cookies with egg white mixture. Press tiny bits of candied cherries on center of knot for holly berries, and make little leaves from the candied citron. Bake at 400° for 10–12 minutes or until set. Do not let brown. Immediately remove from baking sheet.

Sour Cream SPRITZ

1 cup butter
³/₄ cup sugar
1 egg yolk
¹/₃ cup sour cream
1 teaspoon vanilla

³/₄ teaspoon cinnamon
¹/₄ teaspoon baking soda
2³/₄ cups flour, sifted
¹/₂ teaspoon salt

Cream butter and sugar well. Beat in egg yolk, sour cream, and vanilla. Sift dry ingredients and gradually blend into butter mixture. Using cookie press, form cookies on ungreased sheets. Bake at 375° for 8–10 minutes.

Peanut Butter CHOCOLATE

KISS COOKIES

$^1/_2$ cup shortening
$^3/_4$ cup peanut butter
$^1/_3$ cup sugar
$^1/_3$ cup packed brown sugar
1 egg
2 tablespoons milk

1 teaspoon vanilla
1 $^1/_3$ cups flour
1 teaspoon baking soda
$^1/_2$ teaspoon salt
Extra sugar
1 package (6 ounces)
    Hershey's Kisses

Cream shortening and peanut butter. Add sugar and brown sugar. Add egg, milk, and vanilla. Beat well. Combine flour, baking soda, and salt. Gradually add creamed mixture and blend thoroughly. Shape dough into 1-inch balls; roll in sugar. Place on ungreased cookie sheet. Bake 10–12 minutes at 375°. Remove from oven immediately and place an unwrapped kiss on top of each cookie. Remove from cookie sheet and cool.

Traditional NO-BAKE COOKIES

½ cup (1 stick) butter or margarine
½ cup milk
2 cups sugar
½ cup cocoa powder
1 cup peanut butter
1 teaspoon vanilla
3 cups oats

Combine butter, milk, sugar, and cocoa powder in a large saucepan. Bring to a rolling boil. Boil for 3 minutes (do not overboil), and add peanut butter, vanilla, and oats. Drop by heaping teaspoonfuls onto a sheet of waxed paper. Let cool until firm. Store in an airtight container in a cool, dry place.

O Little Town of Bethlehem

O little town of Bethlehem,
how still we see thee lie!
Above thy deep and dreamless sleep
the silent stars go by.
Yet in thy dark streets shineth
the everlasting Light;
The hopes and fears of all the years
are met in thee tonight.

PHILLIPS BROOKS

Applesauce JUMBLES

(From the kitchen of Carolyn Kanow)

The glaze on these cookies enhances the spices, making a yummy treat.

2 eggs
1/2 cup shortening
1 1/2 cups brown sugar
3/4 cup applesauce
2 cups flour
1 teaspoon salt
1/2 teaspoon baking soda

1 teaspoon cinnamon
1/4 teaspoon mace
1/4 teaspoon cloves
1 cup raisins
1 cup chopped nuts
1 teaspoon vanilla

Cream eggs, shortening, sugar, and vanilla. Mix in applesauce. Add all dry ingredients. Cover and chill 2 hours. Drop round teaspoonfuls on ungreased cookie sheet. Bake at 375° for 10 minutes or until there is no indentation when touched. Remove and cool before frosting.

Brown Butter Glaze:

1/2 cup margarine
2 cups powdered sugar

1 1/2 teaspoons vanilla
3–4 tablespoons hot water

Heat margarine over low heat until golden brown. Remove from heat and add vanilla. Sift powdered sugar in and mix well with a whisk. Add water to desired consistency.

Oatmeal MACAROONS

½ cup shortening
½ cup milk
2 cups sugar
½ cup cocoa powder
½ cup flaked coconut
3 cups oats

In a medium saucepan, over medium heat, combine the shortening, milk, and sugar. Bring the mixture to a boil, stirring constantly. Boil for 2 minutes. Remove from heat and stir in cocoa, coconut, and oats; mix well. Drop the mixture by spoonfuls onto waxed paper. Allow to cool for 2–3 hours. Store in an airtight container.

 *Pecan* KISSES

A Christmas favorite!

2 large egg whites
$^3/_4$ cup light brown sugar
$^1/_2$ teaspoon vanilla extract
2 cups pecan halves or pieces

Beat egg whites until stiff peaks form. Gradually beat in brown sugar and vanilla until well blended. Fold in pecans until coated. Drop by teaspoonfuls onto nonstick cookie sheet about 1 inch apart. Bake at 250° for 30 minutes. Turn oven off; let stand in closed oven another 30 minutes. Don't open oven door! Remove from oven and cool on wire rack. Store in airtight container.

Tip: *These cookies freeze well.*

 Chocolate-Toffee COOKIES

(From the kitchen of Andrea Schmidt)

2 ¼ cups flour
1 teaspoon baking soda
1 cup butter
¼ cup sugar
¾ cup brown sugar
1 teaspoon vanilla
1 small package vanilla instant pudding
2 eggs
12 ounces chocolate chips
½ bag toffee bits

Sift flour and baking soda. In separate bowl, mix butter, both sugars, vanilla, and vanilla pudding. Mix until smooth. Beat in eggs. Slowly add flour mixture. Stir in chocolate chips and toffee bits. Bake at 375° for 8–10 minutes.

No-Bake PUDDING COOKIES

2 cups sugar
³/₄ cup butter
¹/₂ (12-ounce) can evaporated milk
1 (3.9-ounce) package instant butter-
    scotch pudding mix
3¹/₂ cups quick-cooking oats

In a medium saucepan, combine the sugar, butter, and evaporated milk. Bring to a boil and allow to boil for 1 minute. Remove from heat and stir in the instant pudding and oatmeal. Spoon the mixture onto a sheet of waxed paper. Allow to cool until firm.

Grandma Peggy's

MOLASSES COOKIES

A family favorite—old-fashioned, timeless.

$^2/_3$ cup shortening
1 cup granulated sugar
1 egg
$^1/_4$ cup molasses
2 cups flour
$^1/_4$ teaspoon salt
$^1/_2$ teaspoon clove
2 teaspoons baking soda
1 teaspoon cinnamon
$^3/_4$ teaspoon ginger

Cream shortening, sugar, and egg. Add molasses and mix well. Add dry ingredients. Roll dough into 1-inch balls and roll in sugar. Bake at 375° for 10–12 minutes until they just flatten out. Watch them closely.

Snowman BUTTER COOKIES

1 cup butter softened (margarine doesn't
   work as well)
$\frac{1}{2}$ cup sugar
$\frac{1}{4}$ teaspoon almond extract
$2\frac{1}{2}$ cups all-purpose flour
1 teaspoon water
Red and green food coloring
Black and orange jimmies or sprinkles

Cream butter, sugar, and extract. Gradually beat in flour and water. Remove $\frac{1}{3}$ cup of mix into small bowls and tint red. Do the same with green; set aside. Shape remaining dough into 12 1-inch balls and 12 $1\frac{1}{2}$-inch balls. Place one smaller ball above one larger ball on ungreased baking sheet; flatten slightly. Use 2 teaspoons of colored dough and form into a hat (make 6 of each color). Place above head. Form scarf from $\frac{1}{4}$ teaspoon of each color into a 3-inch rope. Twist ropes together, leaving one end a little "unraveled." Place scarf around snowman's neck. Insert jimmies for eyes and nose. Bake at 350° for 15–18 minutes or until set. Cool on baking sheets.

There are no great things,

only small things with great love.

Happy are those.

MOTHER TERESA

Chocolate ORANGE BALLS

A quick, easy, no-bake recipe.

1 9-ounce box of vanilla wafer cookies
2 $\frac{1}{4}$ cups confectioners' sugar
$\frac{1}{4}$ cup unsweetened cocoa powder
$\frac{1}{3}$ cup orange juice concentrate
$\frac{1}{4}$ cup light corn syrup
1 teaspoon water
1 $\frac{1}{2}$ cups nuts (Almonds, hazelnuts, or
   pecans work best.)

Combine the vanilla wafers, 2 cups of the confectioners' sugar, cocoa powder, orange juice concentrate, and corn syrup in a food processor. Process until the cookies are ground to crumbs and mixture is evenly blended. If the mixture looks too dry, add water a few drops at a time and blend. Add the nuts and process on "pulse" until the nuts are finely chopped. Transfer the mixture to a bowl and form into 1-inch balls. Roll balls in $\frac{1}{4}$ cup confectioners' sugar to coat. Store in refrigerator in an airtight container for up to 1 month.

Coconut BONBONS

¼ cup butter
1 pound powdered sugar
1 cup sweetened condensed milk
2 cups flaked coconut
9 (1-ounce) squares semisweet chocolate
2 tablespoons shortening

In a medium bowl, combine butter, powdered sugar, and sweetened condensed milk. Stir in the coconut; mix well. Roll the mixture into 1-inch balls. Refrigerate until set, about 1 hour. Melt chocolate and shortening over a double boiler, stirring occasionally until melted and smooth. Remove from heat and stir. Use toothpicks to hold the balls while dipping in the chocolate. Set on waxed paper to dry.

 COOKIES

1 cup butter or margarine, softened
2 cups sugar
1 cup eggnog
1 teaspoon baking soda
$\frac{1}{2}$ teaspoon ground nutmeg
5 $\frac{1}{2}$ cups flour

Beat butter and sugar until fluffy. Add eggnog, baking soda, and nutmeg, and mix well. Gradually add flour, mixing well. Divide dough in half; wrap in plastic. Chill overnight in refrigerator or 2 hours in freezer. On floured surface, roll out half of dough to $\frac{1}{8}$-inch thickness. Cut out with flour-dipped cookie cutters. Place 1 inch apart on ungreased baking sheets. Bake at 375° for 8–10 minutes or until lightly browned. Cool completely, then ice and decorate.

Icing:

3 cups confectioners' sugar $\frac{1}{3}$ cup eggnog
$\frac{1}{4}$ cup butter or margarine, softened

Beat the confectioners' sugar and softened butter until well blended. Gradually beat in $\frac{1}{3}$ cup eggnog until icing is smooth.

Praline COOKIES

12 graham crackers, broken into quarters
1 cup light brown sugar
1 cup butter
1 cup pecan pieces or sliced almonds

Line a baking sheet with aluminum foil and place quarters of graham crackers on it, spaced a little bit apart. Bring brown sugar and butter to a boil and heat into soft-ball stage on a candy thermometer—about 2 minutes after the mixture comes to a full boil. Remove from heat and add pecan pieces or almonds. Pour over the graham crackers and spread nuts evenly among cookies. Bake cookies at 350° for 10 minutes. The mixture will have softened again. Separate into cookies and cool on brown paper. Makes about 48 cookies.

*It was white like coriander seed
and tasted like wafers
made with honey.*

EXODUS 16:31

Christmas SHORTBREAD

1 cup butter
$\frac{1}{4}$ cup sugar
2 cups flour
$1\frac{1}{2}$ cups coconut
$\frac{2}{3}$ cup red or green cherries
$\frac{1}{4}$ cup raisins or currants
$\frac{1}{3}$ cup chopped walnuts or almonds
1 cup Eagle Brand canned milk
Icing sugar

Cream butter and sugar. Blend in flour until mixture resembles coarse crumbs. Pat into greased 9-inch square pan. Bake at 350° for 20 minutes. Combine remaining ingredients. Spread over shortbread and bake an additional 35 minutes or until golden brown. Cool and cut into bars. Dust with icing sugar.

 *Easy* OATMEAL COOKIES

Chewy and crispy!
This is so kid-friendly, children can mix it with their hands!

1 cup butter, softened
1 cup flour
1 teaspoon baking soda
1 cup sugar
2 cups oats

Mix all ingredients together. Dough will form a large ball. Roll into small balls and flatten. Bake at 350° for 12–14 minutes.

Pfeffernusse

3 eggs
½ pound powdered sugar
1 lemon, juice and rind
2 cups flour
¼ teaspoon salt
½ teaspoon baking soda
¼ teaspoon cloves
½ teaspoon cinnamon
¼ teaspoon nutmeg

Beat eggs well. Gradually add powdered sugar, lemon juice, and grated rind. Sift flour, salt, soda, and spices. Sift a second time. Add to egg mixture. Beat to form smooth, medium-soft dough. Chill in refrigerator for several hours. Roll out on floured board into long finger-shaped sticks. Cut into marble-sized pieces. Bake at 425° on greased cookie sheet until light golden brown.

Cinnamon TWISTIES

2 cups sugar
2 cups ground walnuts
1 tablespoon cinnamon
$\frac{1}{2}$ pound butter
$\frac{1}{2}$ pound cream cheese
2$\frac{1}{2}$ cups flour
1 egg, beaten

Mix together sugar, walnuts, and cinnamon and set aside. In another bowl, cream butter and cream cheese together. Gradually add flour. If dough is too soft, add a little more flour. Roll out dough to $\frac{1}{2}$-inch thick and brush with beaten egg. Cover with cinnamon mixture. Cut into 1$\frac{1}{2}$-inch strips and twist. Place on cookie sheet. Bake at 400° for 8–10 minutes.

Brown Sugar COOKIES

Not too sweet—perfect with coffee or tea.

2 cups light brown sugar
1 cup melted butter
3 eggs
$\frac{1}{4}$ cup milk
1 tablespoon vanilla
1 teaspoon baking soda
5–5 $\frac{1}{2}$ cups flour—enough to make
   mixture stiff

Mix ingredients in order given. Add just enough flour to make dough firm enough to roll. Cut into shapes as desired. Decorate with colored sugars, frosting, or sprinkle lightly with brown sugar. Bake at 350° for 8–10 minutes or until edges are lightly browned.

Tip: *This recipe works well with cookie cutters or a cookie press.*

A Babe Is Born in Bethlehem

A Babe is born in Bethlehem, Bethlehem,
Therefore rejoice Jerusalem,
Hallelujah! Hallelujah!
Within a manger He doth lie, He doth lie,
Whose throne is set above the sky.
Hallelujah! Hallelujah!
Stillness was all the manger round, manger round,
The creature its Creator found.
Hallelujah! Hallelujah!
The wise men came, led by the star, by the star,
Gold, myrrh, and incense brought from far.
Hallelujah! Hallelujah!
His mother is the virgin mild, virgin mild,
And He the Father's only Child.
Hallelujah! Hallelujah!

AUTHOR UNKNOWN

Chocolate DATE COOKIES

1 pound graham cracker crumbs
1 (16-ounce) container chocolate frosting
2 tablespoons butter, melted
4 ounces pitted dates, coarsely chopped
¼ cup powdered sugar

In a large bowl, combine graham cracker crumbs, frosting, melted butter, and dates; mix well. Form the mixture into 1-inch balls and roll in the powdered sugar. Store in an airtight container.

Lemon Cardamom COOKIES

 $^1\!/_2$ cup softened butter
 $^1\!/_2$ cup light brown sugar
1 egg
2 cups flour
 $^1\!/_4$ teaspoon salt
 $^1\!/_4$ teaspoon ground cardamom seed
1 $^3\!/_4$ teaspoons grated lemon rind

Cream the butter and sugar until light and fluffy. Beat in egg.
Mix together dry ingredients and stir into butter mixture.
Knead dough briefly and chill. Roll into balls and flatten lightly.
Bake at 350° for 10–12 minutes or until the edges begin to
brown.

Secret KISS COOKIES

(From the kitchen of Shelly Cassara)

> 1 cup butter, softened
> ½ cup granulated sugar
> 1 teaspoon vanilla extract
> 1 ¾ cups flour
> 1 cup finely chopped walnuts
> 1 bag (6 ounces) Hershey's Kisses
> Powdered sugar

Beat butter, sugar, and vanilla until light and fluffy. Add flour and walnuts; mix well. Chill dough 1–2 hours. Remove wrappers from chocolate kisses. Use about 1 tablespoon of dough and shape around chocolate kiss. Roll to make ball. (Be sure to cover chocolate completely.) Bake at 375° for 10–12 minutes. While still slightly warm, roll in powdered sugar.

Vanilla COOKIES

A touch of cardamom makes these cookies extraspecial.

1 cup unsalted butter, softened
1 cup sugar
1 large egg
2 ½ teaspoons vanilla extract
½ teaspoon ground cardamom
½ teaspoon salt
2 ½ cups flour
Vanilla sugar (optional)

Beat butter and sugar until light and fluffy. Beat in egg, vanilla, cardamom, and salt. Mix in flour. Pack dough into cookie press. Fit with desired design plate. Space cookies 1 inch apart on ungreased cookie sheet. Bake at 375° about 10 minutes or until golden brown. Gently transfer cookies to wire racks. If desired, sprinkle with vanilla sugar. Store in airtight container.

Tip: *Place vanilla bean cut lengthwise in 1 cup sugar and store tightly for a day or two. This is also delightful to add to coffees.*

*"Do not work for food that spoils,
but for food that endures to eternal life,
which the Son of Man will give you.
On him God the Father
has placed his seal of approval."*

JOHN 6:27

Swedish PEPPARKAKOR

(From the kitchen of Tracie Peterson)
Swedish pepparkakor are also known as gingersnaps.

1 cup butter (not margarine)
1 ½ cups sugar
1 egg
1 tablespoon dark syrup
3 cups flour, sifted
1 teaspoon baking soda
1 teaspoon ginger
1 teaspoon cloves
2 teaspoons cinnamon

Cream the butter, sugar, egg, and syrup. Sift in the flour, baking soda, and the spices. Cover and chill for at least 2 hours. Roll out and cut with cookie cutter. Bake at 375° for 10 minutes.

Cottage Cheese COOKIES

Though they sound a bit unusual, these are melt-in-your-mouth delicious!

1 cup cottage cheese
2 cubes butter
2 cups flour
3 tablespoons melted butter
$3/4$ cup brown sugar
$3/4$ cup chopped walnuts

Blend together cottage cheese and cubed butter, then add flour. Roll out into a $1/8$-inch-thick circle on floured board. Spread with melted butter. Sprinkle with brown sugar and walnuts. Cut pie-style, then roll from large to small end of wedge like a croissant. Bake at 400° for 10 minutes. Store in sealed tin in refrigerator.

 *Orange* FINGERS

3 ½ cups vanilla wafer crumbs
1 (16-ounce) box powdered sugar, sifted
1 ½ cups chopped pecans
1 (6-ounce) can frozen orange juice
    concentrate, thawed
½ cup butter, melted
1 (7-ounce) package flaked coconut

In a large bowl, combine vanilla wafer crumbs, powdered sugar, and pecans; mix well. Stir in the orange juice and butter. Shape into 2-inch rolls. Roll each piece in the flaked coconut. Refrigerate overnight.

Chocolate CRINKLES

1 cup cocoa
2 cups granulated sugar
2 teaspoons vanilla
$\frac{1}{2}$ teaspoon salt
$\frac{1}{2}$ cup vegetable oil
4 eggs
2 cups flour
2 teaspoons baking powder
Powdered sugar

Combine ingredients, mixing well. Refrigerate overnight. Form balls and roll in powdered sugar. Bake at 350° for 10–12 minutes. Sprinkle with powdered sugar after baking if desired.

French COCONUT MACAROONS

With crisp, chewy outsides and soft centers,
these are popular with children and *grown-ups!*

4 egg whites
1 teaspoon pure vanilla extract
1 cup powdered sugar
2 cups flaked coconut
$\frac{1}{2}$ cup flour

Beat egg whites until stiff peaks form. Add vanilla and mix well. Gradually add in powdered sugar, beating well after each addition. Beat until stiff and glossy. Fold in coconut and flour until well mixed. Drop by teaspoonfuls onto lightly buttered and floured cookie sheet. Bake at 325° for 25 minutes or until lightly browned.

Peanut Butter NO-BAKE COOKIES

2 cups sugar
$^{3}/_{4}$ cup butter
$^{3}/_{4}$ cup milk
$^{1}/_{2}$ teaspoon vanilla extract
$1^{1}/_{2}$ cups peanut butter
$4^{1}/_{2}$ cups quick-cooking oats

In a medium saucepan, over medium heat, combine the sugar, butter, and milk. Bring to a rolling boil and boil for 1 full minute. Remove from heat and stir in the vanilla and peanut butter. Mix in the oats and stir until the mixture begins to cool. Drop the mixture by spoonfuls onto a sheet of waxed paper. Allow to cool until set.

Amnesia COOKIES

2 egg whites
²/₃ cup sugar
1 cup chopped nuts
1 cup chocolate chips

Preheat oven to 350°. Beat eggs until fluffy. Gradually add sugar. Beat until stiff. Stir in nuts and chocolate chips. Drop on foil-lined pan. Put in oven and close door. **Turn oven off!** Do not open oven door until morning!

Grandma Ruth's

FINGER COOKIES

(From the kitchen of Ruth Hermestroff)

These treats are also known as wedding cakes and crescents.

1 cup butter
1 cup flour
1 teaspoon vanilla
1 cup finely chopped pecans
1 teaspoon water
3 tablespoons powdered sugar

Mix all ingredients well and chill for at least an hour. Roll in palm of hand and shape into crescents or roll into balls. Bake at 375° for 10 minutes. Cool and roll in powdered sugar.

Super Chocolate ICEBOX COOKIES

Rich and delicious!

1 ¼ pounds of bittersweet
   chocolate, chopped
¾ cup unsalted butter
1 ⅓ cups sugar
4 large eggs

1 tablespoon vanilla
¾ cup flour
1 ½ cups semisweet
   chocolate chips

Line 8x8 pan with double layer of plastic wrap or waxed paper. Melt chocolate and butter in heavy sauccpan, stirring constantly until smooth. Cool slightly. Whisk in sugar, then eggs and vanilla. Stir in flour. Stir in chocolate chips. Pour dough into prepared pan and smooth evenly. Cover with plastic and refrigerate overnight. Remove from pan and cut dough into 3 even bars (about 2 ½ x 8 inches each). (If making ahead, wrap in plastic and place in freezer bag. Thaw in refrigerator overnight before continuing.) Line baking sheets with baking parchment or Exopat liners. Slice into ½-inch thick slices and space about two inches apart. Bake at 350° for about 15 minutes, or until puffed in center and wrinkled on top. Store in airtight container.

Tip: *Dough can be refrigerated or frozen to bake as needed.*

Sandbakkels

1 cup butter
1 cup sugar
1 egg, slightly beaten
3 cups flour
1 teaspoon vanilla or almond flavoring

Cream together the butter and sugar. Add egg, flour, and vanilla or almond flavoring. Mix well. Chill about 2 hours. Press into metal molds. Bake at 350° for 5–6 minutes, until light brown.

Tip: *These cookies are baked in fluted metal molds, which can be purchased at Scandinavian shops or specialty cooking shops.*

Christmas JOY COOKIES

1 cup of warm memories
1 cup of consideration for others
2 cups of gratitude
1 cup of devotion
2 cups of laughter
3 cups of love

Mix thoroughly.
Flavor with hugs and kisses.
Blend well and fold into daily life.
Bake well with the warmth of human kindness and serve with a smile.

Nuts, Dips, and Mixes

What can I give Him,
Poor as I am?
If I were a shepherd
I would bring a lamb.
If I were a Wise Man
I would do my part.
Yet what can I give Him?
I give Him my heart.

CHRISTINA ROSSETTI

Butterscotch Crispy PARTY MIX

2 cups rice squares cereal
2 cups small pretzel twists
1 cup dry-roasted peanuts
1 cup caramels, unwrapped, coarsely chopped
1 (11-ounce) package butterscotch chips

Coat a 9x13-inch baking pan with nonstick cooking spray. In a large bowl, combine the cereal, pretzel twists, peanuts, and caramels. Place the butterscotch chips in a medium microwave-safe bowl. Microwave at high (100%) for 1 minute; stir. Microwave an additional 10–20 seconds or until smooth when stirred. Pour over the cereal mixture; stir to coat evenly. Spread the mixture into the prepared baking pan; let stand for 20–30 minutes or until mixture is firm. Break apart into small pieces.

Cashew CRUNCH

2 cups milk chocolate chips
¾ cup chopped cashews
¾ cup chopped macadamia nuts
½ cup (1 stick) butter, softened
½ cup sugar
2 tablespoons light corn syrup

Line a 9-inch square pan with aluminum foil, extending the foil over the edges of the pan. Butter the foil. Cover the bottom of the pan with chocolate chips. Combine the cashews, macadamia nuts, butter, sugar, and corn syrup in a large skillet. Cook over low heat. Stir constantly until the butter is melted and the sugar is dissolved. Increase the heat to medium. Stir constantly until the mixture begins to cling together and turns brown. Pour the mixture over the chocolate chips. Cool until firm. Remove from the pan and peel off the foil. Break into pieces. Store in an airtight container in a cool, dry place. Makes about ½ pound.

Caramel FRUIT DIP

1 (8-ounce) package cream cheese
$\frac{1}{4}$ cup honey
$\frac{1}{2}$ cup caramel topping
$\frac{1}{4}$ teaspoon cinnamon

Let cream cheese soften in a medium-sized mixing bowl about 15 minutes, or until mixer can blend it easily. Add remaining ingredients and beat until smooth and creamy. Serve with fresh fruit.

Sweet PARTY MIX

1 (12-ounce) package crispy corn and rice cereal
5 ounces slivered almonds
6 ounces toasted, chopped pecans
$\frac{3}{4}$ cup butter
$\frac{3}{4}$ cup dark corn syrup
1 $\frac{1}{2}$ cups light brown sugar

Preheat oven to 250°. Lightly grease a large roasting pan. In a large bowl, mix cereal, almonds, and pecans. In a medium saucepan, over medium heat, melt the butter and add corn syrup and brown sugar; stir. Pour the butter mixture over the cereal mixture; toss to coat evenly. Pour the mixture into the prepared pan. Bake for 1 hour, stirring every 15 minutes. Allow to cool and store in an airtight container.

Christmas FRUIT DIP

1 (7-ounce) jar marshmallow cream
1/4 cup powdered sugar
1 tablespoon lemon juice
(8-ounce) package cream cheese, softened

In a medium bowl, beat all ingredients together until well blended. Serve as a party dip. Arrange whole or sliced fruits on a party tray around the bowl of dip.

I wish we could put up some of

the Christmas spirit in jars

and open a jar of it every month.

HARLAN MILLER

Cherry JUBILEE COOKIES JAR MIX

$^1\!/_2$ cup plus 2 tablespoons flour
$^1\!/_2$ cup rolled oats
$^1\!/_2$ cup flour mixed with $^1\!/_2$ teaspoon baking soda
$^1\!/_2$ teaspoon salt
$^1\!/_3$ cup white sugar
$^1\!/_3$ cup plus 1 tablespoon packed brown sugar
$^1\!/_2$ cup dried cherries
$^1\!/_2$ cup slivered almonds

Layer the ingredients in a quart jar in order as listed. Attach recipe that follows to jar:

Cherry Jubilee Cookies:

In a medium bowl, cream together:

$^1\!/_2$ cup butter   1 egg
1 teaspoon vanilla

Add the entire jar of ingredients. Mix together by hand until well blended. Drop by heaping spoonfuls onto greased baking sheet. Bake at 350° for 8–10 minutes.

 SPICED NUTS

3 cups pecan halves
1 cup sugar
1/3 cup orange juice
1 tablespoon ground cinnamon
1/2 teaspoon salt
1/2 teaspoon ground cloves

Spread the pecans over the bottom of a 10x15x1-inch pan. Toast at 275° for 10 minutes. Remove from the oven and set aside. In a medium saucepan, combine the sugar, orange juice, cinnamon, salt, and ground cloves. Over medium heat, cook and stir until heat reaches the soft-ball stage. Remove from heat and stir in the pecans. Remove the pecans from the pan and spread onto waxed paper. Separate and let dry for 2 hours. Store in an airtight container.

White Chocolate CHERRY CRUNCH

2 cups corn squares cereal
2 cups miniature pretzels
2 cups dry-roasted peanuts
1 cup miniature marshmallows
1 (3-ounce) package dried cherries
1 (12-ounce) package white chocolate chips
$\frac{1}{4}$ cup half-and-half
$\frac{1}{4}$ teaspoon almond extract

In a large bowl, combine the cereal, pretzels, peanuts, marsh-mallows, and cherries; set aside. In a large saucepan, over low heat, cook chocolate chips and half-and-half, stirring constantly until chips are melted. Stir in the almond extract. Pour the melted mixture over the dry ingredients. Toss gently until the dry ingredients are evenly coated. Drop the mixture by spoon-fuls onto a sheet of waxed paper. Let stand about 1 hour or until set. Store loosely covered up to one week.

GIFT *Ideas*

- Heavily starch a doily and drape it over the bottom of an overturned bowl until it's dry and stiff. Fill with shortbread and tie with tartan ribbon.

- Oversized coffee mugs, antique china cups and saucers, and whimsical trays are easy to fill and give away. It's fun to add sample-sized packets of gourmet coffee or tea to them.

- Cellophane-wrap a bunch of cookies and tuck it into a flower pot for an avid gardener. Tuck in a package of flower seeds, too.

Molasses COOKIE MIX

These old-fashioned chewy, spicy cookies are delightful.

Layer in a 1-quart jar:

2 cups flour
1 teaspoon baking soda
1 teaspoon cinnamon
$1/4$ teaspoon cloves
1 teaspoon ginger

1 cup sugar
1 teaspoon baking powder
$1/2$ teaspoon nutmeg
$1/8$ teaspoon allspice

Attach recipe that follows to jar:

Molasses Cookies:

Preheat oven to 375°. In large bowl, mix:

$3/4$ cup butter or margarine,
   softened

$1/4$ cup sulfured molasses
1 egg

Add the cookie mix; beat until smooth. Shape the dough into 1-inch balls. Roll in granulated sugar. Place 2 inches apart on ungreased cookie sheets. Bake for 9–11 minutes. Cool on wire racks.

 SNACK MIX

2 cups salted peanuts
$\frac{1}{2}$ cup whole almonds
$\frac{1}{2}$ cup cashews
$\frac{1}{2}$ cup chopped dates
$\frac{1}{2}$ cup red and green candy-coated chocolate pieces
$\frac{1}{2}$ cup raisins
2 tablespoons shelled sunflower seeds

Combine all ingredients in a large bowl; mix well. Store in an airtight container in a cool, dry place.

Fruit SALSA

2 kiwifruit, peeled and diced
2 apples, peeled, cored, and diced
8 ounces raspberries
1 pound strawberries
2 tablespoons powdered sugar
1 tablespoon brown sugar, firmly packed
3 tablespoons fruit preserves, any flavor

In a large bowl, mix kiwifruit, apples, raspberries, strawberries, powdered sugar, brown sugar, and fruit preserves. Cover and refrigerate. Serve with cinnamon chips (see page 303 for recipe).

Cinnamon CHIPS

10 (10-inch) flour tortillas
2 cups cinnamon sugar
Butter-flavored cooking spray

Preheat oven to 350°. Coat one side of each flour tortilla with the butter-flavored cooking spray. Cut the tortillas into wedges and arrange them in a single layer on a large cookie sheet. Sprinkle the wedges with the cinnamon sugar. Spray them once more with the butter-flavored cooking spray. Bake for 8–10 minutes. Repeat the process with any remaining tortilla wedges. Allow to cool for at least 15 minutes. Serve with the fruit salsa (see page 302 for recipe).

Blueberry HAZELNUT DREAMS

JAR MIX

½ cup plus 2 tablespoons flour
½ cup rolled oats
½ cup flour mixed with
    ½ teaspoon baking soda
½ teaspoon salt

⅓ cup plus 1 tablespoon
    packed brown sugar
⅓ cup white sugar
½ cup hazelnut pieces
½ cup dried blueberries

Layer the ingredients in a quart jar in order as listed. Attach recipe that follows to jar:

Blueberry Hazelnut Dreams:

In a medium bowl, cream together:

½ cup butter
1 teaspoon vanilla

1 egg

Add the entire jar of ingredients. Mix together by hand until well blended. Drop by heaping spoonfuls onto greased baking sheet. Bake at 350° for 8–10 minutes.

Granola BITES

1 cup powdered sugar
1 cup creamy peanut butter
$^1/_3$ cup milk
1 teaspoon vanilla extract
1 $^1/_2$ cups oats
1 cup granola cereal
1 $^3/_4$ cups (11-ounce package) peanut
    butter and milk chocolate chips

Line two baking sheets with waxed paper. In a large bowl, combine powdered sugar, peanut butter, milk, and vanilla; mix well. Stir in the oats, cereal, and chips. Mix until the cereal is evenly coated. Roll the mixture into 1-inch balls and place on the prepared baking sheets. Let stand until firm. Store in an airtight container.

Do what you can,

with what you have,

where you are.

THEODORE ROOSEVELT

Christmas PARTY MIX

2 cups miniature pretzels
2 cups chow mein noodles
2 cups crispy corn squares cereal
1 cup peanuts
1 cup raisins
3 egg whites
1 ½ cups sugar
1 teaspoon ground cinnamon
1 teaspoon salt
1 large package candy-coated chocolate
    pieces

Preheat oven to 225°. Grease a cookie sheet; set aside. In a large bowl, combine the pretzels, chow mein noodles, cereal, peanuts, and raisins. In a medium bowl, beat egg whites until foamy. Stir in the sugar, cinnamon, and salt. Pour over the pretzel mixture, and stir until evenly coated. Spread onto prepared cookie sheet. Bake for 1 hour, turning mix with a spatula every 15 minutes. Allow to cool completely. Stir in the chocolate pieces. Store in an airtight container in a cool, dry place.

Peanut Butter and Chocolate
COOKIE JAR MIX

Layer in a one-quart jar:

$^3/_4$ cup sugar

$1^3/_4$ cups flour

$^1/_2$ teaspoon baking soda

$^1/_2$ cup brown sugar

1 teaspoon baking powder

8 Reeses' peanut butter cups, chopped into chunks

Attach recipe that follows to jar:

Peanut Butter and Chocolate Cookies:

Sift out the peanut butter cup chunks and set aside. Empty remaining cookie mix into large mixing bowl and stir with fork. Add:

$^1/_2$ cup butter softened at room temperature

1 egg, slightly beaten

1 teaspoon vanilla

Mix until completely blended. Mix in peanut butter cup chunks. Shape into $1^1/_2$-inch balls. Place 2 inches apart on greased cookie sheets. Bake at 375° for 12–14 minutes. Cool 5 minutes on baking sheet. Remove cookies to racks to finish cooling.

 PECAN BITES

1 pound pecan halves
2 egg whites, stiffly beaten
1 cup sugar
Pinch of salt
$\frac{1}{2}$ cup butter

Preheat oven to 275°. Place the pecans on a cookie sheet and toast for 10–15 minutes; set aside to cool. Place egg whites in a medium bowl. Fold in sugar, salt, butter, and the toasted pecans. Increase oven temperature to 325°. Grease the cookie sheet and spread the pecan mixture over it. Bake for 30 minutes, stirring every 10 minutes. Allow to cool completely before serving.

Vanilla PARTY MIX

1 (10-ounce) package miniature pretzels
5 cups rice squares cereal
1 (1-pound) package candy-coated chocolate pieces
2 (12-ounce) packages vanilla chips
3 tablespoons vegetable oil

In a large bowl, combine pretzels, cereal, and chocolate pieces; set aside. In a small, microwave-safe bowl, combine chips and vegetable oil. Microwave on high (100%) for 2 minutes. Stir, and microwave at high for 10 more seconds. Stir until smooth. Pour over cereal mixture and mix well. Spread onto waxed paper and allow to cool completely. Store in an airtight container in a cool, dry place.

Caramel POPCORN

3 quarts popcorn, popped
3 cups mixed nuts, unsalted
1 cup brown sugar, firmly packed
$\frac{1}{2}$ cup light corn syrup
$\frac{1}{2}$ cup margarine
$\frac{1}{2}$ teaspoon salt
$\frac{1}{2}$ teaspoon baking soda
$\frac{1}{2}$ teaspoon vanilla extract

Preheat oven to 250°. In a large roasting pan, combine the popcorn and nuts. Place pan in the oven while preparing the glaze. In a medium saucepan, combine brown sugar, corn syrup, margarine, and salt. Bring to a boil over medium heat, stirring constantly. Boil for 4 minutes without stirring. Remove from heat; stir in baking soda and vanilla. Pour the mixture over the warm popcorn and nuts, tossing to coat evenly. Bake another 60 minutes, stirring every 10–15 minutes. Cool and break apart. Store in an airtight container.

True happiness comes from

the joy of deeds well done,

the zest of creating things new.

ANTOINE DE SAINT-EXUPERY

Polka Dot OATMEAL COOKIES

JAR MIX

1/2 cup packed brown sugar

1/4 cup white sugar

3/4 cup wheat germ

1 cup quick-cooking oats

1/4 cup dried cherries

1/2 cup raisins

2/3 cup packed flaked coconut

1/4 cup dried cranberries

1 cup flour

1/2 teaspoon salt

1/2 teaspoon baking soda

Layer ingredients in order given in a quart jar. Attach recipe that follows to jar:

Polka Dot Oatmeal Cookies:

Empty the jar into a large bowl. Blend mixture well before adding: 1/2 cup of softened butter. Mix until mixture resembles coarse crumbs. In separate bowl, beat together:

1 egg

1/4 cup milk

1 teaspoon vanilla

Blend egg mixture into the dough until well combined. Bake on greased cookie sheet at 350° for 10–14 minutes.

Macadamia CLUSTERS

8 ounces vanilla chips
$^1/_2$ tablespoon orange zest
2 (3$^1/_2$-ounce) packages macadamia nuts

Place the vanilla chips in a microwave-safe bowl. Microwave uncovered on high (100%) for 40–60 seconds. Stir until melted and smooth. Stir in nuts and orange zest. Drop mixture by teaspoonfuls onto a sheet of waxed paper. Allow to cool until set. Store in an airtight container in a cool, dry place.

Pumpkin DIP

1 (8-ounce) package cream cheese, softened
2 cups powdered sugar
1 (15-ounce) can solid-pack pumpkin
1 tablespoon ground cinnamon
1 tablespoon pumpkin pie spice
1 teaspoon frozen orange juice concentrate

In a medium bowl, combine cream cheese and sugar; mix until smooth. Stir in the pumpkin. Add the cinnamon, pumpkin pie spice, and orange juice. Mix until well blended. Chill in the refrigerator 1 hour before serving. Hollow a miniature pumpkin and place dip inside just before serving. Serve with apple wedges and gingersnaps.

Christmas Tree DIP

1 (8-ounce) package cream cheese, softened
1 yellow bell pepper
1 (2-inch) piece green onion
¼ cup salsa
¼ cup apricot preserves
1 teaspoon fresh cilantro, chopped

Cut the block of cream cheese diagonally in half. Arrange the cut cream cheese triangles on a serving plate to form a tree. Cut a star shape out of the bell pepper with a small star-shaped cookie cutter. Place the star at the top of the tree. Place the green onion piece at the bottom of the tree to form the trunk. In a small bowl, mix together the salsa and the apricot preserves. Spoon the mixture over the cream cheese tree. Sprinkle cilantro over the tree. Serve with tortilla chips or crackers.

 Glazed NUTS

1 egg white
½ cup brown sugar, packed
2 tablespoons ground cinnamon
1 teaspoon ground cloves
1 teaspoon ground ginger
1 tablespoon vanilla extract
1 cup walnut halves
1 cup pecans
1 cup almonds

Preheat oven to 300°. Spray a cookie sheet with nonstick cooking spray. In a large bowl, beat egg white until foamy. Stir in the brown sugar, cinnamon, cloves, ginger, and vanilla. Add the nuts; stir to coat. Spread evenly onto the prepared cookie sheet. Bake for 30 minutes, stirring occasionally, until golden brown. Allow to cool completely. Store in an airtight container.

Brownies BY THE QUART

Layer in a one-quart jar:

2¼ cups white sugar   1¼ cups flour
⅔ cup cocoa   1 teaspoon baking powder
½ cup chopped nuts   1 teaspoon salt

Attach recipe that follows to jar:

Brownies by the Quart:

Empty mix into large bowl. Mix thoroughly. In a small bowl, mix:

¾ cup of butter   4 slightly beaten eggs

Add butter and egg mixture to dry ingredients and stir well with fork. Spread batter into a lightly greased 9x13-inch pan. Bake at 350° for 30 minutes or until done.

*Each man should give what
he has decided in his heart to give,
not reluctantly or under compulsion,
for God loves a cheerful giver.*

2 CORINTHIANS 9:7

Pineapple CREAM CHEESE DIP

2 (8-ounce) packages cream cheese, softened
1 cup minced celery
$\frac{1}{2}$ cup green bell pepper, chopped
1 teaspoon minced onion
1 (20-ounce) can crushed pineapple, drained
1 cup chopped pecans

In a medium mixing bowl, combine cream cheese, celery, bell pepper, onion, and crushed pineapple; mix well. Stir in the chopped pecans. Chill in the refrigerator overnight. Serve with crackers.

Cinnamon-Roasted ALMONDS

1 egg white
1 teaspoon cold water
4 cups whole almonds
$^1/_2$ cup sugar
$^1/_4$ teaspoon salt
$^1/_2$ teaspoon ground cinnamon

Preheat oven to 250°. Lightly grease a 10x15x1-inch pan. Lightly beat the egg white; add water, and beat until frothy but not stiff. Add the almonds and stir until well coated. In a small bowl, combine the sugar, salt, and cinnamon; sprinkle over the almonds. Toss to coat, and spread evenly on the prepared pan. Bake for 1 hour, stirring occasionally, until golden. Allow to cool completely. Store in an airtight container.

Chunky CHOCOLATE MACADAMIAS JAR MIX

Layer in a wide-mouthed one-quart jar:

> $^3/_4$ cup brown sugar (Pack firmly in jar.)
> $^1/_4$ cup unsweetened cocoa powder
>   (Wipe any smears off inside jar.)
> $1^3/_4$ cups flour
> 1 teaspoon baking powder
> $^1/_2$ cup white sugar
> $^1/_2$ cup chopped macadamias
> 1 cup jumbo chocolate chips
> 1 teaspoon baking soda
> $^1/_4$ teaspoon salt

Attach recipe that follows to jar:

Chunky Chocolate Macadamias:

Empty jar of cookie mix into a large mixing bowl. Mix dry ingredients with spoon. Add:

> $^3/_4$ cup butter softened at room temperature.
>   (Margarine does not work.)
> 1 egg, slightly beaten
> 1 teaspoon vanilla

Mix until completely blended. The dough is thick and sticky. You'll need to finish mixing with your hands. Shape into walnut-sized balls and place 2 inches apart on parchment-lined baking sheets. Do not use waxed paper. Bake at 350° for 11–13 minutes. Cool 5 minutes on baking sheet. Remove to racks to finish cooling.

Honey Yogurt FRUIT DIP

1 container vanilla yogurt
3 tablespoons honey
Fresh fruit such as apples, pears, grapes,
    strawberries, and kiwifruit

Place the yogurt in medium bowl; whisk until smooth. Stir in the honey, leaving a marbled effect. Cut the fruit into wedges or bite-sized pieces, or leave whole. Arrange the fruit on a platter with the bowl of dip in the center. Serve chilled.

Christmas CHEESE BALL

(8-ounce) cream cheese
4 ounces blue cheese
1 tablespoon green pepper, chopped
1 tablespoon diced pimento
Chopped walnuts
Minced parsley

In a medium bowl, combine cream cheese, blue cheese, green pepper, and pimento. Roll into a ball. Roll the ball in the chopped walnuts. Garnish with parsley and serve with crackers.

Strawberry FRUIT DIP

1 (8-ounce) package strawberry-flavored cream cheese
1 (7-ounce) jar marshmallow crème

In a medium mixing bowl, mix the cream cheese and marshmallow crème until well blended. Chill at least one hour before serving. Serve with your favorite fruit.

I will honor Christmas in my heart,

and try to keep it all the year.

CHARLES DICKENS

 COOKIE JAR MIX

Layer in a 1-quart jar:

1 ⅓ cups quick oats
½ cup sugar
1 cup chocolate chips
1 teaspoon baking powder
2 dashes salt

½ cup firmly packed brown
    sugar
½ cup chopped pecans
1 ⅓ cups flour mixed with
    1 teaspoon baking soda

Attach recipe that follows to jar:

Cowboy Cookie Mix:

Empty jar into a large mixing bowl; blend mix together. Add:

1 stick butter, melted
1 teaspoon vanilla

1 egg, slightly beaten

Mix until thoroughly blended. Shape generous teaspoon-sized balls 2 inches apart on greased cookie sheet. Bake at 350° for 11–13 minutes until edges are lightly browned. Cool 5 minutes on baking sheet, then remove cookies to racks to finish cooling.

White Chocolate CHRISTMAS MIX

2 pounds white chocolate
3 cups toasted oat cereal
2 cups cashews
6 cups crispy rice squares cereal
2 cups thin pretzel sticks
1 (12-ounce) package miniature candy-coated
    chocolate pieces

Melt white chocolate in a large saucepan over low heat or in microwave just until soft. Stir until completely melted. Combine all the other ingredients in a large bowl. Pour melted white chocolate over mixture; stir until evenly coated. Turn out onto waxed paper. Allow to cool. Break into pieces.

Chocolate Chip CHEESE BALL

1 (8-ounce) package cream cheese, softened
1/2 cup butter, softened
3/4 cup powdered sugar
2 tablespoons brown sugar, firmly packed
1/4 teaspoon vanilla extract
3/4 cup miniature semisweet chocolate chips
3/4 cup finely chopped pecans

In a medium bowl, combine cream cheese and butter. Beat with an electric hand mixer, on low speed, until smooth. Stir in powdered sugar, brown sugar, and vanilla. Add chocolate chips; stir. Cover and refrigerate for 2 hours. Form the chilled mixture into the shape of a ball. Wrap in plastic wrap and refrigerate for another hour. Roll the ball in the chopped pecans. Keep refrigerated until ready to serve.

Spiced MIXED NUTS

1 egg white, lightly beaten
1 teaspoon water
1 (8-ounce) jar dry-roasted peanuts
½ cup blanched whole almonds
½ cup pecan halves
¾ cup sugar
1 tablespoon pumpkin pie spice

In a large bowl, combine egg white and water. Add nuts; toss to coat. Combine sugar and spice; sprinkle over the nuts and toss until well coated. Place nuts in a single layer on lightly greased baking sheet. Bake at 300° for 20–25 minutes. Immediately transfer the nuts to waxed paper. Allow to cool. Break up any large clusters. Store in an airtight container.

Sand Art BROWNIES

JAR MIX

A fun gift to put together!

Layer in 1-quart jar:

½ cup plus 2 teaspoons flour
⅓ cup cocoa
⅔ cup brown sugar
½ cup semisweet chocolate chips
½ cup walnuts and pecan pieces

⅔ teaspoon salt
½ cup flour
⅔ cup sugar
½ cup vanilla
    baking chips

Attach recipe that follows to jar:

Sand Art Brownies:

Add:

1 teaspoon vanilla
1 egg

⅓ cup oil
⅓ cup warm water

Bake at 350°:

9x9-inch pan 27–33 minutes
7x11-inch pan 32–37 minutes

Ginger FRUIT DIP

1 (3-ounce) package instant vanilla pudding mix
1 ½ cups milk
1 (6-ounce) can frozen orange juice concentrate
¼ cup sour cream
¼ teaspoon ginger

In a medium bowl, combine pudding mix, milk, and orange juice concentrate; mix well for 1 minute. Stir in sour cream and ginger. Chill several hours to blend flavors. Serve with fresh fruit for dipping.

Roasted PUMPKIN SEEDS

1 ½ cups raw whole pumpkin seeds
2 teaspoons butter, melted
Pinch of salt

Preheat oven to 300°. In a small bowl, toss seeds with melted butter and salt. Spread the seeds in a single layer on a cookie sheet. Bake for 45–50 minutes or until golden brown, stirring occasionally. Allow to cool before serving. Hollow a miniature pumpkin and place roasted seeds inside just before serving.

Pumpernickel SPINACH DIP

1 (8-ounce) container sour cream
$\frac{1}{2}$ (8-ounce) package cream cheese, softened
2 tablespoons mayonnaise
1 (1-ounce) package dill dip mix
$\frac{1}{2}$ bunch spinach, rinsed and chopped
1 (8-ounce) round pumpernickel loaf

In a medium bowl, combine the sour cream, cream cheese, mayonnaise, dill dip mix, and spinach; mix well. Cut out the center of the pumpernickel loaf, creating a bowl. Cut the removed bread into bite-sized squares. Fill the hollowed loaf with the spinach dip. Serve with the pumpernickel squares.

S'more MIX

2 cups honey or cinnamon graham cereal
$^1/_2$ cup milk chocolate chips
1 cup salted peanuts
1 cup miniature marshmallows
$^1/_2$ cup raisins

Combine all ingredients in a large, festive bowl.

A Christmas Cookie Blessing

May your cookie jar always be half full—
Because you've shared some with your family.
May you have good friends
with whom to share most of the rest.
But in the middle of the night
When you cannot sleep,
May there always be two left
For when you chat with the Almighty.

Other Tasty Treats

Now that the time has come wherein

Our Savior Christ was born,

The larder's full of beef and pork,

The granary's full of corn.

As God hath plenty to thee sent,

Take comfort of thy labors,

And let it never thee repent

To feed thy needy neighbors.

AUTHOR UNKNOWN

 PUFFS

Puffs:

¼ cup melted butter

½ cup sugar

½ cup milk

1 egg, slightly beaten

1½ cups flour

1 tablespoon baking powder

Pinch salt

½ teaspoon cinnamon

1 cup apples, peeled and
  finely chopped

Topping:

¼ cup sugar

½ teaspoon cinnamon

¼ cup finely chopped walnuts

1 apple, peeled and thinly
  sliced

Combine butter and sugar. Stir in milk and egg. Add flour, baking powder, salt, and cinnamon. Stir just enough to mix. Fold in chopped apples. Spoon batter into greased muffin cups. Mix sugar, cinnamon, and walnuts and sprinkle evenly over muffins, then top each with an apple slice. Bake at 350° for 20 minutes.

Mocha Meringue KISSES

These are heart smart!

3 egg whites
$1/4$ teaspoon cream of tartar
$2/3$ cup sugar
$1/2$ teaspoon vanilla
2 teaspoons cornstarch
1 tablespoon crushed instant coffee
$1/4$ cup finely chopped almonds

Beat egg whites with cream of tartar until frothy; gradually add $1/3$ cup sugar and beat until stiff. Add vanilla. Mix $1/3$ cup with cornstarch, coffee powder, and nuts. Fold in egg whites. Spoon into parchment paper-lined baking sheets. Bake in preheated 300° oven for 30 minutes. Turn off oven. Allow these to cool in oven. Tops should be dry and slightly browned. Variation: Use cocoa powder instead of instant coffee.

Chocolate Strawberry

MOUSSE DELIGHT

Chocolate Base:

$\frac{1}{2}$ cup shortening

3 squares unsweetened chocolate

1 $\frac{1}{4}$ cups sugar

1 teaspoon vanilla

3 eggs

$\frac{2}{3}$ cup flour

$\frac{1}{2}$ teaspoon baking powder

$\frac{1}{4}$ teaspoon salt

Melt shortening and chocolate in pan on low heat, stirring until smooth. Remove from heat. Add sugar, vanilla, and eggs. Mix well. Combine flour, baking powder, and salt. Add to chocolate mixture and stir until well blended. Spread into a greased 9-inch spring form pan. Bake at 350° for 25–30 minutes.

Topping:

> 1 package frozen sliced strawberries with
>   syrup
> 1 pouch gelatin
> $\frac{1}{2}$ cup sugar
> 2 tablespoons lemon juice
> 2 cups whipping cream
> Fresh strawberries for garnish, if desired

Drain strawberries and reserve liquid. Add water to make $1\frac{1}{4}$ cups of liquid. Combine gelatin and sugar in pan. Stir in strawberry liquid and lemon juice. Bring to boil. Stir constantly to dissolve sugar and gelatin. Remove from heat and chill until starting to set. Beat $1\frac{1}{4}$ cups of the whipping cream to stiff peaks. Beat gelatin mix with electric mixer until light. Fold into whipped cream. Fold in drained strawberries. Spread evenly over base in pan and chill until set, approx $1\frac{1}{2}$ hours or overnight. To serve, beat remaining whipping cream to stiff peaks and garnish with fresh strawberries if desired.

Cherry CHRISTMAS DESSERT

1 (21-ounce) can cherry pie filling
1 (8-ounce) container whipped cream
1 (14-ounce) can sweetened condensed milk
1 (10-ounce) can crushed pineapple, drained
1 package cherry gelatin mix, dry
½ cup chopped nuts

Combine all ingredients above in a large bowl; mix well. Refrigerate for at least 4 hours before serving.

Unless we make Christmas

an occasion to share our blessings,

all the snow in Alaska

won't make it "white."

BING CROSBY

Old-Fashioned

CHRISTMAS PUDDING

2 cups fresh bread crumbs
$^3/_4$ cup milk
2 eggs, well beaten
1 cup suet, finely chopped
$^1/_2$ teaspoon salt
1 cup brown sugar
1 cup flour
$^1/_4$ teaspoon allspice
$^1/_4$ teaspoon nutmeg
1 teaspoon cinnamon
1 teaspoon baking powder
$^1/_4$ teaspoon baking soda
1 cup raisins
1 cup orange peel
$^1/_2$ cup dates and cherries, chopped
1 apple, peeled
1 cup chopped walnuts
$^1/_2$ cup dark molasses
1 teaspoon lemon peel

In a large bowl, combine bread crumbs with milk, and let soak until moist. Add beaten eggs, chopped suet, salt, brown sugar, and flour. Add spices and all other ingredients, and mix well. Divide into two round balls. Tie in cheesecloth. Place a metal cookie cutter into a cooking pan. Pour in water to measure 1½ inches. Set pudding on top of cookie cutter. Cover pan and heat water to boiling over high heat. Reduce heat to low and simmer pudding until toothpick inserted through cheesecloth comes out clean. Serve warm with hard sauce.

Hard Sauce:

> 2 cups sugar   2 cups water

Cook and thicken with cornstarch. Add dash of salt to taste. Serve warm over Old-Fashioned Christmas Pudding.

Lemon Cream DESSERT

$^1/_2$ cup butter
1 package vanilla wafers, crushed
1 6-ounce frozen lemonade concentrate, thawed
1 can Eagle Brand milk
1 pint whipping cream, whipped

Melt butter; add crushed vanilla wafers. Press into 9x9-pan. Save some for topping. Chill. Mix lemonade, milk, and whipped cream. Spread over base; sprinkle with reserved crumbs. Refrigerate 24 hours before serving.

Chocolate Rainbow ROLLS

½ cup (1 stick) butter or margarine
2 cups (12-ounce package) semisweet
    chocolate chips
6 cups (10½-ounce package)
    miniature colored marshmallows
1 cup finely chopped nuts
Additional chopped nuts

In a medium saucepan, over low heat, melt the butter and the chocolate chips until blended, stirring constantly. Remove from heat and cool for 5 minutes. Stir in the marshmallows and 1 cup of nuts. Do not let the marshmallows melt. On a sheet of waxed paper, shape the mixture into two 7-inch rolls. Wrap the rolls in aluminum foil and refrigerate for about 20–25 minutes. To coat the rolls, roll them in the additional nuts. Wrap and refrigerate overnight. Cut the rolls into ¼-inch slices. Store in an airtight container in a cool, dry place. Makes about 3 dozen slices.

Cherries JUBILEE

Mixture 1:

> 2 cups graham wafer crumbs (¼ set aside)
> ⅓ cup butter or margarine
> 1 can cherry pie filling

Mixture 2:

> ½ pint whipping cream, whipped
> 1 package mini marshmallows

To assemble:

Put all of Mixture 1 in 13x9-inch pan. Cover with half can of cherry pie filling. Put half of Mixture 2 on top of filling. Cover with the rest of the cherry pie filling. Use the second half of Mixture 2. Top with remaining crumbs. Chill and serve.

Caramel APPLE BITES

6 individually wrapped caramels,
  unwrapped and chopped
2 tablespoons light corn syrup
2 apples, peeled, cored, and diced

Combine the caramels and corn syrup in a medium, microwave-safe bowl. Microwave on high (100%) for about 30 seconds or until melted. Put the apples in the bowl and toss until coated with the caramel mixture. Allow to cool 10 minutes before serving.

Festive FRUIT KABOBS

½ (20-ounce) can sliced pineapple in juice,
    drained
16 seedless red grapes
16 toothpicks
16 seedless green grapes
1 (10-ounce) jar maraschino cherries, drained

Cut pineapple slices into eighths. Thread any combination of 4–5 pieces
of fruit on each of 16 toothpicks. Serve with your favorite fruit dip.

Cranberry STORM

1 cup graham crumbs
¼ cup butter, melted
1 small package cranberry jelly powder
½ cup whole cranberry sauce
Rind of 1 orange
Peeled sections of 1 orange
1 tub (4 cups) thawed Cool Whip

Mix crumbs and butter into 9-inch square pan; set aside. Mix jelly powder with ⅔ cup boiling water, then 1 cup cold water. Stir in cranberry sauce, orange rind, and orange sections. Fold in Cool Whip. Chill until slightly thickened, about 10 minutes. Spoon into crust. Freezes well.

Coffee Chocolate DESSERT

Graham cracker squares (not crumbs)
1 pint whipping cream (2 cups)
$1/2$ cup icing sugar
4 tablespoons liquid chocolate
1 tablespoon instant dry coffee
Chocolate decoration—shaved chocolate
    or chocolate sprinkles
Sundae topping

Place layer of graham crackers in 9x9-inch pan. Whip cream; add next 3 ingredients. Place $1/3$ of mixture on crackers. Repeat with crackers then add second $1/3$ of the mixture, top with crackers, then last $1/3$ of the mixture. Sprinkle top with chocolate decoration.

Raspberry CREAM CAKE

1 package raspberry jelly powder
$\frac{1}{2}$ cup boiling water
6 large ice cubes
1 cup whipping cream

Put jelly powder and water in blender on high for 15 seconds. Add ice and blend on high until the ice is gone. Pour in whipping cream and blend for a few seconds. Pour into individual serving dishes. Chill.

Good news from heaven the angels bring,

Glad tidings to the earth they sing:

To us this day a child is given,

To crown us with the joy of heaven.

MARTIN LUTHER

 *Caramel* RAISIN PUDDING

1 ½ cups boiling water	½ cup brown sugar
2 teaspoons butter	¼ teaspoon vanilla

Combine and boil for 5 minutes. Pour hot syrup into buttered baking dish. Set aside.

½ cup seedless raisins	1 teaspoon baking powder
¼ cup milk	¼ teaspoon salt
¾ cup flour	2 teaspoons butter

Soak raisins in water for 5 minutes. Drain; stir in milk. Combine flour, baking powder, salt, and butter. Add raisins and milk. Drop batter from spoon over hot sauce. Bake at 350° for 25–30 minutes. Serve warm.

Holiday DESSERT

1 (3.9-ounce) package pistachio instant pudding mix
1 (1-pound) can crushed pineapple
1 (8-ounce) container whipped cream
1 cup miniature marshmallows

In a large bowl, combine the pudding mix and the pineapple. Add whipped cream and marshmallows; stir well. Refrigerate for 1 hour before serving.

Cool Christmas STRIPES

1 4-ounce package green jelly powder
1 package Knox gelatin
$\frac{1}{2}$ cup cold water
$\frac{3}{4}$ cup sugar
1 cup whipping cream
1 cup sour cream
1 teaspoon vanilla
1 4-ounce package red jelly powder
1 cup boiling water
1 15-ounce can blueberries with juice

Can be made in a large bowl or individual clear dessert/parfait glasses.

First layer: Prepare green jelly powder according to directions on box. Place in large bowl or in individual clear serving glasses (each $\frac{1}{3}$ full).

Second layer: Mix gelatin with $\frac{1}{2}$ cup cold water in saucepan. Heat to dissolve but do not boil. Add sugar. Cool. Whip cream and mix with sour cream and vanilla. Mix with the gelatin mixture; pour over first layer.

Third layer: Dissolve red jelly powder with 1 cup boiling water (not according to directions). Add can of blueberries and the juice and pour over the second layer. Let stand in fridge for several hours before serving.

 SURPRISE

1 cup flour
1 teaspoon sugar
$^1/_8$ teaspoon salt
2 teaspoons baking powder
$^1/_2$ cup milk
1 cup chopped apple

1 cup brown sugar
1 tablespoon lemon juice
1 $^1/_2$ cups boiling water
2 tablespoons butter
$^1/_2$ teaspoon cinnamon

Mix dry ingredients, add milk, then work in chopped apple. Spread this mixture evenly in the bottom of a greased baking dish. Blend brown sugar, lemon juice, boiling water, and butter. Pour over batter. Sprinkle cinnamon on top. Bake at 375° for 20–25 minutes. When done the sauce will be bubbling underneath.

 Peach DELIGHT

Base:

1¼ cups graham crumbs

¼ cup sugar

⅓ cup melted butter

Filling:

12 ounces softened cream cheese

½ cup sugar

Almond extract to taste

Topping:

2 cups peach pie filling (or your choice)

3 tablespoons softened butter

½ cup flour

¼ cup brown sugar

½ cup sliced almonds

Mix base and press into 9x13-inch pan. Bake at 375° for 8 minutes. Chill 1 hour in fridge. Mix filling and spread on base. Spread pie filling on top of this mixture. Combine flour, sugar, and butter. Mix well. Stir in almonds. Sprinkle over fruit filling. Bake at 375° for 25–30 minutes or until golden brown. When cooled completely, cut into 15 squares and top each square with ½ peach.

Broken Glass DESSERT

Base:

1½ cups graham wafer crumbs   ⅓ cup butter, melted

⅓ cup sugar   1 teaspoon cinnamon

Filling:

1 3-ounce package red jelly powder

1 3-ounce package lime jelly powder

1 3-ounce package lemon jelly powder

4½ cups hot water, divided

2½ cups whipping cream

½ cup sugar

1 envelope unflavored gelatin

½ cup cold water

½ cup hot water

¼ cup pineapple juice

Mix together ingredients for base. Press into 13x9-inch pan and chill. Dissolve each jelly powder in 1½ cups hot water. Pour into separate pans; chill and cut into ½-inch cubes. Whip cream; add sugar. Soften gelatin in the ½ cup cold water; dissolve in hot water and add pineapple juice. When cool, combine with whipped cream mixture. Add whipped cream/gelatin mix to jelly cubes. Pour into chilled crust. Chill. Makes 12 or more servings.

Creamy JELLY LAYERS

1 small package jelly powder (lime, cherry, or any
dark color)
1 ½ cups boiling water
2 cups frozen Cool Whip (reserve remainder of container for topping)

Dissolve jelly powder in boiling water. When jelly powder is dissolved, immediately whisk in frozen Cool Whip and pour into
individual see-through serving containers. Chill until set. This
separates into 2 layers. When set, top with unused thawed Cool
Whip (must be set enough so the Cool Whip will not sink).
Serves 4.

Black Forest TRIFLE

1 package Fudge Cake
1 large package instant chocolate pudding
1 quart cherry pie filling
$^3/_4$ quart whipping cream
Chocolate curls
Maraschino cherries

Prepare and bake Fudge Cake in 2 layers, then slice into chunks. Prepare chocolate pudding. In a large bowl, layer chunks of chocolate cake, pudding, pie filling, and whipping cream—making 3 repetitions and ending with a layer of cake and cream. Garnish with whipping cream, chocolate curls, and cherries. Chill and serve.

Christmas DESSERT PUDDING

4 (14-ounce) cans sweetened condensed milk
4 pints heavy whipping cream
1 (4-ounce) jar maraschino cherries
1 cup chopped almonds

Remove the labels from the cans of sweetened condensed milk and put them unopened into a large pot of gently boiling water. Allow to boil for about 3 hours. Make sure the water doesn't boil away. After 3 hours, take the cans out and chill in the refrigerator. When chilled, open the cans and put the contents into a large bowl. In a medium bowl, beat the whipping cream until thick, and fold into the bowl of sweetened condensed milk. Stir in the cherries and almonds.

*"He has shown kindness by giving you
rain from heaven and crops in their seasons;
he provides you with plenty of food
and fills your hearts with joy."*

ACTS 14:17

Chocolate DELIGHT

1 package (4 serving size) instant chocolate pudding
2 cups milk
2 cups Cool Whip, thawed
Chocolate garnish (chocolate chips, grated chocolate,
    chocolate cookie crumbs, or garnish with straw-
    berries instead)

Prepare pudding with milk as directed on package. Fold 1½ cups Cool Whip topping into pudding; spoon into 4 dessert dishes. Top with remaining ½ cup Cool Whip and chocolate garnish.

FROZEN *Peanut Butter* MOUSSE

1 egg white
¼ cup sugar
1 cup heavy cream
½ cup creamy peanut butter
½ cup milk

¼ cup light corn syrup
Dash salt
Spray-type whipped cream
4 maraschino cherries,
    with stems

Beat egg white into soft peaks, then add sugar and beat into stiff peaks. Set aside. Beat cream until stiff; set aside. Beat peanut butter and milk until smooth. Mix in corn syrup and salt until well blended. Fold egg white mixture and cream mixture into peanut butter mixture until smooth and well blended. Pour into eight 4-ounce serving cups or one 1-quart bowl. Cover and freeze until firm, about 1 hour for small cups, 3 hours for single container. To serve, remove from freezer and let stand in fridge for 10 minutes (30 minutes for single container). Garnish with spray-style whipped cream and maraschino cherry.

 CHERRY DESSERT

Base:

    2 cups crushed graham wafers   ½ cup melted butter
    6 tablespoons icing sugar

Combine and line a 9x12-inch pan, reserving 2 tablespoons for sprinkling on top.

Filling:

    2 small cartons whipping cream   1 can cherry pie filling
    1 package mini marshmallows

Whip the cream and fold in marshmallows. Put ½ onto base. Cover with pie filling and top with remaining whipped cream mixture. Top with reserved crumbs. Set in fridge for two days prior to serving.

Chocolate TRIFLE

1 chocolate cake mix, and ingredients
1 cup cold coffee
6 Skor chocolate bars
1 instant chocolate pudding mix
1 small tub Cool Whip

Make 1 chocolate cake mix according to directions. Bake. Cut into chunks and sprinkle coffee over top. Break up chocolate bars into fine pieces. Make chocolate pudding according to directions; add half the Skor pieces, then add to cake pieces. Top with Cool Whip, then top with the rest of the Skor pieces.

Pineapple SUPREME

2 cups graham cracker crumbs
$^1/_3$ cup butter or margarine
1 large container sour cream
2 large cans crushed pineapple
2 4-ounce packages vanilla instant pudding

Mix crumbs and butter and press into bottom of 13x9-inch pan. Mix remaining ingredients and pour over graham wafer crust. Chill until set.

Pistachio REFRIGERATOR DESSERT

40 Ritz crackers, crushed (or chocolate wafers)
$\frac{1}{2}$ cup butter or margarine
2 boxes pistachio instant pudding
1 $\frac{1}{2}$ cups milk
4 cups vanilla ice cream
Whipping cream or any dessert topping
Nuts (optional)
Chocolate shavings (optional)

Mix crumbs and butter and pat into a 9x13-inch pan. Bake at 350° for 10 minutes; cool. Mix pistachio pudding with milk and ice cream. Blend well. Spread on baked base. Top with whipped topping and garnish with nuts or shaved chocolate. Place in freezer. To serve, let sit at room temperature for approximately 30 minutes.

Rainbow RIBBONS

Takes a long time to prepare, but it's worth it!

5 single packages jelly powder, any colors
1 cup plain or vanilla yogurt
6 ¼ cups boiling water

Dissolve 1 package jelly powder in 1 ¼ cups water. Pour ¾ cup of this mixture into an 8-cup ring mold. Chill until set but not firm, about 15 minutes. At the same time, chill remaining jelly in bowl until slightly thickened. Gradually blend in 3 tablespoons yogurt. Pour over jelly in mold. Note: Instead of pouring onto the jelly, pour onto a spoon to "splash" it on. Chill until set but not firm, about 15 minutes. Repeat with remaining jelly, making layers. When assembled, chill until firm, about 2 hours. To unmold, dip mold into warm water for 10 seconds. Place serving plate on top of mold; invert onto plate.

 *Chocolate* MOUSSE

1 envelope gelatin (unflavored)
$\frac{1}{4}$ cup sugar
1 cup semisweet chocolate chips
4 eggs, separated
$\frac{1}{4}$ teaspoon salt
$\frac{1}{3}$ cup sugar
2 cups whipping cream
2 toffee candy bars, chopped
Chocolate wafers

In a medium saucepan, add $\frac{1}{4}$ cup of water. Dissolve the gelatin and $\frac{1}{4}$ cup sugar in the water over low heat. Stir in the chocolate chips until melted. Remove from the heat and beat in the egg yolks one at a time. Cool in a covered bowl for 10–15 minutes. In a separate bowl, add egg whites and salt. Beat until mixture has soft peaks. Beat $\frac{1}{3}$ cup of sugar into the egg whites. Carefully fold the egg whites into the chocolate mixture. In a separate bowl, add the whipping cream and whip until it becomes thicker and is creating soft peaks. Fold half of the whipped cream into the chocolate mixture. Place a large spoonful of mousse in a parfait glass, followed by a spoonful of candy and whipped cream. Repeat for each layer. Top with whipped cream and serve with chocolate wafers.

Quick Cherry DESSERT

1 cup butter
1 ½ cups sugar
4 eggs
1 teaspoon almond extract
2 cups flour
2 tablespoons baking powder
1 21-ounce cherry pie filling
Powdered sugar to dust on top
Whipped cream to spread on top

Cream butter and sugar; add eggs, beat until light and fluffy. Add extract, stir in flour and baking powder; mix until smooth. Turn into buttered 13x9-inch pan. Spoon pie filling onto cake in 16 spots, spacing 4 across and 4 down evenly. Bake at 350° for 45–50 minutes or until done. Filling will sink into cake while baking. To serve, cut into 16 pieces. Place bottom side up on plate; dust with powdered sugar if desired and spoon whipped cream over each serving. Great served warm.

*"Glory to God in the highest,
and on earth peace to men."*

LUKE 2:14

Baked Lemon SPONGE PUDDING

2 medium eggs, separated
2 tablespoons butter or margarine
¾ cup sugar
3 tablespoons flour
1 tablespoon grated lemon rind
¼ cup fresh lemon juice
Pinch salt
1½ cups milk

Beat egg whites and set aside. Cream butter and sugar together. Add egg yolks and beat well. Stir in everything else except the egg whites and mix well. Fold beaten egg whites into mixture and pour into buttered 1½-quart baking dish and place in pan of hot water. Bake at 350° for 45 minutes. Makes 4–6 servings.

Very Easy TRIFLE

1 package strawberry jelly powder
3 tablespoons custard powder
3 tablespoons sugar
2½ cups milk
1 angel food cake, made according to
    package directions
1 can fruit cocktail, drained
1 package strawberries, drained
1 pint whipping cream, whipped

Prepare jelly powder according to package directions, reducing water by ½ cup. Cool and set. Cut into 1-inch cubes. Set aside. Mix custard powder and sugar. Gradually add milk and cook, stirring over medium heat. When it comes to a boil, remove from heat; set aside to cool. Cut angel food cake into 1-inch squares. Set aside. Drain fruit cocktail and strawberries. Pat dry with a paper towel. Set aside. Layer as follows 3 times: (1) cake pieces, (2) custard, (3) jelly squares, (4) fruit, (5) whipped cream. After third repetition, garnish with a few strawberries. Chill. Serve.

Whip 'n Chill

STRAWBERRY DESSERT

1 cup graham crumbs
⅓ cup butter
1 package strawberry Whip 'n Chill
1 package frozen strawberries, not drained
1 package strawberry jelly powder

Combine crumbs and butter to make a crust; press into bottom of 9x9-inch pan. Over this, spread Whip 'n Chill. Let set 1 hour in fridge. Heat liquid from frozen strawberries, adding jelly powder to this instead of water. Cool and pour over Whip 'n Chill. Put in fridge to set. Top with whipped cream.

Cranberry, Chocolate, Orange

ROUNDS

2 cups raw cranberries, chopped
½ cup sugar
3½ cups flour
1½ cups sugar
1 teaspoon baking powder
1 teaspoon baking soda
1 teaspoon salt

2 eggs
1½ cups orange juice
¼ cup oil
1 tablespoon grated orange
   rind
2 cups semisweet
   chocolate chips
1 cup chopped nuts

Combine cranberries and ½ cup sugar and set aside. Combine 1½ cups sugar and balance of dry ingredients. Beat eggs, juice, oil, and rind together and add to dry ingredients; stir just until moistened. Fold in cranberries, chocolate chips, and nuts. Divide batter into 8 or 9 well-greased 10-ounce soup cans. Fill just over half full and bake at 350° for 35–40 minutes or until done. Cool 10 minutes then run blade of thin knife around edges of tin to loosen. Turn out on rack to cool completely. Wrap and store overnight before slicing or freeze for later use.

Raspberry ROLL

Syrup:

    1 cup brown sugar   1 cup water

Boil for 10 minutes. Set aside.

Biscuit dough:

2 cups flour	4 teaspoons baking powder
½ cup milk	4 tablespoons shortening
1 teaspoon salt	Butter for spreading

    1 package frozen raspberries, drained and patted dry

Make biscuit dough and roll ½–inch thick. Spread with raspberries. Roll like a jelly roll. Cut into 1½–inch slices. Lightly butter each slice and cover with syrup. Bake at 350° for 25–30 minutes.

Cheesecake PUDDING

1 (8-ounce) package cream cheese, softened
1 stick butter
1 cup powdered sugar
2 (3.9-ounce) boxes instant vanilla pudding mix
3 cups milk
1 small container frozen whipped topping,
    thawed
3 cups chocolate sandwich cookies, crushed

In a large bowl, mix cream cheese, butter, and powdered sugar until well blended. In a separate bowl, combine pudding mix and milk; mix well. Add the whipped topping. Pour the pudding mixture into the cream cheese mixture and stir until completely blended. In parfait glasses, layer crushed cookies and pudding mixture, ending with the crushed cookies. Continue filling glasses until mixture is gone.

Peanut Butter LOGS

1 cup peanut butter
2 cups icing sugar
1 cup chopped walnuts
1 cup chopped dates
4 squares semisweet chocolate, melted
Shredded coconut

Mix like a pastry and roll dough into a small log. Dip or roll in chocolate and roll in coconut. If dough is too stiff to roll, add a little coffee or milk.

*"For God so loved the world
that he gave his one and only Son,
that whoever believes in him
shall not perish
but have eternal life."*